BEYOND THE ENCHANTED
...Ever After

BY CHERYL JACOBS

BEST SELLING AUTHOR of "Escape from the Darkness into the Enchanted"

Published By

"I Am a Published Author" The Lifestyle Publishing Company for *Women*

http://www.myiaapa.com

info@myiaapa.com

Copyright 2018 © All Rights Reserved

This book and all graphics is protected by International Copyright Law and nothing within this book may be copied or used for any purpose without express permission of the author.

About Cheryl Jacobs

Born & raised near Cleveland, Ohio. I got married at 18, had 2 beautiful children & divorced at 21. During my divorce, I lived in poverty so poor I had to go to the local church for milk & cheese to feed my 2 babies. Shortly after my mother passed of breast cancer @ the young age of 43 & my grandmother passed away 3 months later. It was the darkest time of my life.

My life was forever changed. The words of my mother saying, "Never depend on anyone & always have the capability to stand on your own 2 feet" was the driving force behind me. Soon I graduated from Kent State University in aeronautical engineering w honors. Started my 1st business a modeling & talent agency. Slowly but surely, I began to heal from all the tragedy in my life.

I then landed a huge modeling contract with Playboy Book of Lingerie. No nudity!!! This changed my life. I then bought my 1st home & a fishing charter boat & started my 2nd business.

Eventually my modeling & acting career really took off. I moved to LA & NY to pursue it in full swing. I ended up selling everything in Ohio & moving to NYC. I landed over 50 roles on "Law & Order" & the "Sopranos" Enough to pay my rent in 5 days of work. My resume now consists of over 36 TV & film appearances as well as several print jobs like Romance book covers, catalogs, runway etc.

These days I'm starting my now 8th business branding my company KidsPartyCharacters.com & taking it nationwide & hopefully international. Plus, I'm a pilot working with the owners of Netjets since 2005. Yes, I can teach you to fly a plane.

My goal is to help people to see no matter what life throws at you it can be overcome with hard work & drive.

Media Contact and Party Information

MEDIA AND CONTACT FOR KID'S PARTY CHARACTERS

Website: http://www.kidspartycharacters.com
Facebook: https://www.facebook.com/kidspartycharactersny/
Twitter: https://twitter.com/PartyCharacter
LinkedIn: https://www.linkedin.com/in/cheryl-jacobs-348b7650/
Instagram: https://www.instagram.com/cherylejacobs/
Pinterest: https://www.pinterest.com/chezr1sque/

Contents

Introduction	xi
Building Your Dream	*xi*
## The beginning	1
## Journal Entries	3
Beyond the Enchanted	*3*
## Podcasting & Blogging	7
Starting My Blog	*8*
My Mentor and Business Vision	*9*
## Relationships and Love	10
New Relationships	*10*
Surprise visit to Ohio	*11*
## Business Mastery	14
Back to Working on my Business	*14*
Tony Robbins	*15*
My Morning Routine	*18*
The loneliness of Entrepreneurs	*19*
Business Mastery	*20*
Day 1 Tony Robbins	*21*
Tony Robbins and Sales Reps	*21*
Business Financials with Tony Robbins	*21*
Return from Tony Robbins	*22*
Back to NJ after Tony Robbins	*23*
Reflection	*24*
Launch of Kids Party Characters Podcast	*24*
Meeting of the Minds with my Copilots	*24*

A New Sort of Relationship (Florida Bound)	25
Life's Struggles	26
The girls of BM	27
My 1st real biz partner	27
Florida Bound Again…	28
Launching of his book	29
Me in the back filming it all.	30
Back to NYC	30
Another Let Down	30
Flight Club	32
What is Your Why	33

The Interviews 37

Meet My Heroes	37
Podcast Guest AJ Mihrzad	56
Bumi Veyg	87
DJ Dove	124
Jose Baez	134

INTRODUCTION

Building Your Dream

Beyond the Enchanted is Cheryl Jacob's 2nd published book. A series of journal entries and enchanted plans as she is learning how to become a better business owner, while expanding her flight experience and speaking voice, this book shows you that no matter where you come from, you can do and be anything you want to become.

Cheryl Jacobs is a #1 Bestselling Author and Co-Author who has spent her entire life, growing from a young mother who encountered many unique life lessons on her journey, to a highly successful business coach and professional pilot. Her first book "Out of the Darkness into the Enchanted" detailed her journey from finding herself a single mom, to creating multiple business brands including "Kid's Party Characters", a highly successful business that brings happiness and joy to children, and her actors are all passionate about what they do as well.

"In life we have choices. Different forks in the road. Not knowing which way to turn. It's that fear of the unknown that often keeps us from our full potential. Fear of failure, fear of success, fear of what others will say. It's at times of adversity which propels us to find that strength. Through my journey of the unknown I have been reborn into a new me. A new path of strength. A new path of love & adventure."

How to Read this Book

This book is part raw journal entries, part transcription of Cheryl's podcast for her brand messaging. The latter chapters reveal her talent to talk to people and celebrate them as valuable members of her life's journey. Cheryl continues to grow and expand her company, her brand and her message that everyone is worthy of achieving any dream they may have, and she encourages young people to stay in school and build their dreams.

Keep in mind that this book has been compiled from journal entries and real-life interviews from the podcast, as such, it's raw and unedited in the spaces of journal entry.

THE BEGINNING

"The Only Way to Begin a Path to Success is to Take Steps Toward Your Biggest Dreams"

I have kept a journal for as long as I can recall. I decided to preserve the journal entries in this autobiography. Life seems to have sped up and taken many turns since my first book was released. I have to admit that the first book was a bit harder than I thought, as I revealed parts of my life that nobody had ever known before. Pulling out those parts of my life caused me to be fearful, perhaps of what others though, but mainly because it caused me to revisit some really painful times in my life; many forks in the road from pulling out of the fire of pain and falling into an enchanted life and business.

In my first book I talk about how I started my company Kid's Party Characters and where I was headed with the company. I revealed some areas of my personal past that involved my children, and some areas that focused on my past relationships. I want to start you out in this book with some of my journal entries and end up with the transcripts from my podcast that I host to help give people a place to raise their voices.

Please note, the journal entries are not edited for the purpose of preserving my voice. I have written lessons and stories for you to assist you in understanding and absorbing the free thoughts of my journal entries.

I also want to guide you on my journey "Beyond the Enchanted" so you can see the choices I made on the path to running 4 successful businesses. Since my first book, I have taken Kid's Party Characters into many more locations and have started my franchise opportunity to help women who are sick of the corporate grinds, step into a business that allows them the total freedom to create something magical rather than mundane, with the time they have left on earth.

JOURNAL ENTRIES

Beyond the Enchanted

Start: The journey continues. I find myself in a position of power. Not like the almighty but on the verge of something bigger than myself.

"Never be afraid of the word POWER. It's there for those who can use it for good to help others." Cheryl

For the last year of my life taking my kid's company through its branding process was just the beginning. Little did I know the branding would take 9 months out of my life. Finally, the launch last week & now the marketing begins.

I joined a Facebook group called "Coffee with Dan" which is all about entrepreneurs who give each other tips and help each other with networking. I found I wasn't alone in the entrepreneurial world. I made many friends and colleagues I would have never gotten without joining the group. 1 by 1 I hired a podcast expert, a franchise expert claiming to take my business to a 5000% increase at franchise shows, let's see about that, and people who have helped me with copywriting and infotainment.

The founder Dan personally taught me how to make memes on a train ride back to Brighton.

My trip to the UK was amazing. I set up a photoshoot with a photographer I found on my Model Mayhem Portfolio at http://www.modelmayhem.com/CherylJ

I dressed like Elsa from the movie "Frozen" and shot by the Tower Bridge which image would later be used for the cover of this book. I met a brilliant podcast coach and copywriter for a meeting of the minds who showed me the West Minster Aby and a few other land marks.

I also joined a private flight club called "Wingly" where I will be flying to when we launch Kids Party Characters London. I am now working with an amazing PR lady whom I had the opportunity to meet in TX w/ her wife. Love her!!!

I have a Facebook & Instagram expert I keep in contact with them both who have been marketing my membership site on both social medias. I am currently working with mentors who are keeping me accountable for business actions. More to come on that.

1 even wanted to set me up on a dating site. Saying I need balance in my life. Being alone doing this is 1 thing I struggle a lot with. I can write a whole chapter on that subject.

Anyways time to entertain the kiddies. End

Part of what I do for the Kid's Party Character company is get dressed up in costume and go entertain the children, watching their eyes sparkle like stars when they see their favorite character at a birthday party or other celebration. On the cover of this book, I am Elsa from the Disney movie "Frozen". Giving full credit to Disney for this amazing movie, I have to say that playing Elsa truly changed my life and connected me with so many hopeful children.

My trip to London/UK was simply magical.

Since my business started, I have encountered my share of heartache and have hit rock bottom, emotionally, more than once. Starting the company was a big move for me, but one that was worth it beyond words.

Granted, being a successful entrepreneur can come with its share of loneliness but doing the work and showing up is worth every bit of the battle.

In my first book, I detailed with you, my life as a model and an actor; a broken and beautiful journey. I have always been told I was beautiful by everyone. While that is an amazing feeling, one of the life changes I had to make to get to where I was then, to where I am now, is to embrace all aspects of myself: I am also very intelligent. But – that's our little secret ok?

Ever After…

As I journey through my satisfying and magical life, I am reminded of how I got here. This is no Cinderella story, but is a story of how I made my way. Education was always important.

As far as education goes, I graduated from Kent State University in aeronautical engineering with honors. I also had the honor of attending the Lee Strasburg Institute and studied at Carnegie Hall. This was an interesting time in my life. I made 30 appearances on the Sopranos as the Bartender to the "BadaBing" and about 20 appearances in Law and Order as well as starred in 15 films, TV Appearances, Romance Book Covers, Several Costume and Bridal Catalogs and Print ads.

Little did I know that I was creating my future through the steps I made during a volatile time in my life. Acting gave me the foundation to go out and be a children's character and make children all over the world – happy. I also attended flight school against the odds. Learning to fly, at that time in my life, helped take away the pain and confusion of not knowing what my future held.

PODCASTING & BLOGGING

Today my podcast helps me practice my speaking voice for my future speaking tour on my books and my branding vision. Podcasts, as you may or may not know, are ways you can consume content through audio, driving in your car or falling asleep. Interviewing some amazing people gave me insight into how others life and start companies.

I started the podcast for two reasons:

1. To practice my speaking voice and;
2. To help others have their voice be celebrated.

At the end of this book, you will find the transcripts of my podcast with some pretty amazing people. Each one of them has been instrumental in my growth to higher understandings of humanity and the lessons we are taught each day.

You may think that actors have speaking voices, but that could be no further from the truth. Public speaking is the #1 fear of everyone and I am no exception. Podcasting is a great way to do this thing called speaking, without feeling the heat of the room, and the faces looking at you.

Starting My Blog

Entry:

I started my blog. The biggest challenge is coming up with the free value and checklists. Once I get going it's all about experiences I've already had. I'm sharing it with others.

As I go through this journey of learning and implementing into my business along the way I finally really feel alive. Like I have a purpose to let as many families know there's a way to bring so much joy to your kids and through others in a way a lot know nothing about. It's a business but it's all about the kids.

End of Entry

This year (2018) we witnessed millions of kids all over the USA, leaving their schools in protest of gun control laws and issues. Every day, the news reported more kids marching and voicing their opinions about guns and violence in their schools. Their plea was strong as they were fearing for their very life.

When I can go into a home and see small children, I get to show them the way of happiness and joy. Hopefully, my work has touched the life of a child, so they grow up feeling validated, accepted and loved. Doing this work makes my heart feel so good and helps me become more creative in my goals. Seeing children laughing and believing in the magic of life, gives me happiness beyond words.

My Mentor and Business Vision

I have always been taught to do what I can do, and to hire people to do what I can't do. This lesson was part of my business development for the past two years and will continue to be part of all future plans I have for my companies. I have attended many workshops and events, including Tony Robbins Business Mastery where I learned so much about how to run my business.

The most important choice I made was to get a mentor to hold me accountable, and to manage my growing team of actors, admins, web designer, branding and PR professionals and more. I have to admit that I was a one woman show in Kid's Party Characters in the beginning but quickly realized that success cannot be created on your own. You need a mentor and a coach to help hold your feet to the fire when it comes to success in a business venture.

> *Entry: I now I have in place a mentor who's gonna be holding myself and my team accountable for doing things properly and getting shit done.*
>
> *She will be stepping into the poor progress my last team has done. Also, I have a marketing genius who's been working on the front end of my membership site. Over the next 3 months it will all consist of 7am meetings with the UK, copywriting, making blogs and filming for my new podcast & YouTube channels.*

My franchise expert has set up a convention in March for Chicago & London. This is where I will be bringing my sales rep & an actress to dress up like a princess each day. We are hoping to sell 10 memberships per show. Now writing blogs & copywriting is a new skill I've been developing over the last 2 months. I think I'm ready to start having it bring value to the people.

I also just hired a meme king & graphic designer to make all my banners & memes for growing my business.

END of ENTRY

RELATIONSHIPS AND LOVE

New Relationships

In my book "Out of the Darkness – Into the Enchanted" I poured out my soul about past relationships and how I felt like I was a victim of narcissism and other relationship killing episodes, but the truth is, these were all lessons. Knowing what I know today, I am 100% confident that there is someone for me, and that I won't settle, until I find him.

In anyone's walk through life, they will have relationships that come, and they go. My own stories of failed relationships are different that yours; but they are all similar, would you agree? There are certain conditions that we place upon others which are truly harmful.

The #MeToo movement brought out 1000's if not millions of stories from women who raised their voices about being raped, assaulted or abused by men. This is not just a man thing. This is an epidemic across the board. Abuse and Assault are two areas of human rights which still must be talked about.

I deeply desire to have a companion, but I am more vigilant in choosing the men I allow to be near me. You will see me say "my boy" throughout this book, which usually means I am talking about someone I am dating or seeing.

> *Finally met an adorable man & had a 1st date. So far so good but hard to tell where it will lead. Of course, he's younger by 12 years. Always manage to get those tall, dark, young and handsome guys.*
>
> *Anyways time to create magic on my 1st podcast Intro recording.*

Surprise visit to Ohio

When I left Ohio all those years ago, I left my family behind to pursue my dreams and goals of being an Actress/Model and learning to fly a plane. I had one goal in mind: To do whatever I had to do, to become more than I had ever been. I love going home to see my family, especially my grandchildren.

My son had a hard time dealing with my decision to pursue my dreams and he and I have since come to forgiveness and understanding.

I planned on a surprise visit to Ohio to see my Christmas. Telling only my father I was doing so. I hadn't been home to visit for Christmas in 10 years. I've always been working or simply couldn't afford to do so.

I would normally go home after the 1st of the year when biz was slow & it was cheaper to travel.

It wasn't easy to keep it a secret. I sent about $150 home for my daughter & promised to send a gift home for her boys. My son a week prior had asked for money yet once again. I had been sending him $1000's of dollars for many years.

He had put a guilt trip on for moving away for many years. The truth is I hate living in Ohio. It's not me. People never change. They do the same things year after year, century after century. The kids I grew up with all doing menial jobs with zero goals. Popping kid after kids out with little expectations to ever break away from that cycle. Not what I ever wanted for my life.

It upsets some people that I went out to pursue my dreams. Especially my son. It was a constant battle with him between the heroin, cocaine, marijuana & alcohol.

They say this is a disease. BS you choose your path. I took much abuse from his manipulations about sending him money to see him turn around & spend it on material things for girls or drugs.

This time to Ohio was the final straw. I have been through enough mental & verbal abuse with him and had to give some tough love. I have such a hard time communicating with him. It's a struggle that deeply bothers me. It's so painful watching someone you love to turn onto someone you don't even know.

A lot of guys these days want to sit in front of the computer playing video games & getting high instead of working then blame the world for their problems. I refuse to be an enabler.

The entire world doesn't owe you. The more you dwell on the past you will never move forward. There is no excuse for not being successful. Keep your head on straight. Stop blaming the world. Get your ass in gear & start working hard day after day. Then you collaborate. Not a second before. NO ONE OWES YOU!!!

I want to leave you some strategies and action steps for being in good, healthy relationships. These tips are going to help you stay clear of men (or women) who have no intention on giving you what you crave. I can honestly say that I am lonely a lot, and that I deeply desire a loving relationship, but I am also true to myself. Your story of finding enchantment, will always be filled with relationship issues.

#1 Find someone you can talk to for hours on end with a two-way conversation that last for hours. Listen to them intently and reply to their words.

#2 Always keep gentle boundaries as it related to sexuality and intimacy. You may want to jump their bones but ask yourself the questions of your boundaries.

#3 If it feels uncomfortable, it's not right. Your gut is trying to alert you to possible trouble.

BUSINESS MASTERY

Back to Working on my Business

Starting my podcast was not just about me, but it was about learning how people think about their own life and business. I interviewed the key players in my life that have helped me through many hurdles to get to where I am today. I have put a lot of time into my business and my life in general.

I became highly addicted to self-help and personal development. The Tony Robbins conference I attended opened my mind up to the possibility of being a high paid business leader and the courage to see myself as "In Power". Fearless leaders must accept their power, to be able to fulfill their duties to a public – needing their services.

> The 1st real day back to work. Thank God. Today was Podcast building, followed by completing my Tony Robbins final payment for Business Mastery & setting up my registration with the Chicago convention. Followed by assignments by my mentor, YouTube training & reading a chapter of "A Brand called You'
>
> Building my Podcast started by signing up for a Libsyn account & iTunes account which I already had for the numerous kids' songs I've downloaded for partied. The start of the training with my coach I felt a little overwhelmed by it all. He patiently walked me through how to do a zoom interview & set up my Mic.

1 by 1 I invited all the guests willing to participate on the podcast launch. In a day my 1st mentor Mell Martin, my ghost writer Carla Wynn Hall, my animated commercial artist Rohan Vale & my Podcast coach Scott Doucet all set up interviews for next week.

A lot to follow. End of January is my marketing expert Jonny Cooper, my friend & supplement chef Bumi Veyg, my dear friend & ex BF who is an amazingly successful Online Supercoach AJ Mihrzad, my top actor & supermodel Jose Emilio Baez who's been with us since day 1.

This is gonna either break me or make me. I'm gonna fight with all my might to give my babies a good life.

On a mission to bring joy to as many children & their families across the globe.

Tony Robbins

I was given several worksheets to complete during the Tony Robbins event that I want to share with you now. Believe it or not, doing these exercises will help you grow your mental muscles and become a leader in your own life's purpose. Tony Robbins holds nothing back when he tries to break you down to your greatness.

TRY TO ANSWER THESE SAME QUESTIONS FOR YOURSELF AND SEE WHAT YOU COME UP WITH.

1) What is something you tend to focus on that doesn't serve you? **These are my answers below!**

- Men who make me an option instead of a priority

- How to change my son's opinion of me

- Wasting time & energy on people who don't give results

- Letting go of the past

2) What's something you do on a regular basis that you really don't need to do?

- Spend too much time on social media

3) What's something you really want for your life?

- A real assistant, which I believe I have now

- Someone who can run my business, so I can focus on flying or family

- Financial freedom

- A loving boyfriend

4) Why must you master the RPM life management? (RPM Results-focused, Purpose-driven, Massive action plan)

- Results keep focused on team building & on franchising

- Purpose is to bring joy to as many kids & their families as possible

- Give my children & grandchildren financial freedom

- Massive Action

a) Start interviewing assistants

b) Find a plane that's usable

c) Find a partner

d) Eliminate people who aren't on the same journey

Getting to know me. you will start to see that it's my diversity and multi-faceted way I look at love, relationships and success. I believe everyone has grand potential to be anything they want to be, and for those who don't like how they are – then tough. It took me years to grow beyond the Enchanted to who I am today, and let me tell you, I am hard on myself. I have to keep my (nearly 50-year-old) body, in shape so I can continue making kids smile with my kid's company.

My Morning Routine

Time to walk the dog & hit the gym. My morning routine 4-5 days a week.

1st 8am meeting with my marketing coach Jonny Cooper via zoom from the UK. Today we decided to make my company into franchises which we would later call territories. We upped the membership fee from $2000 to $10,000 which include the starter costume package.

Joining ½ way through the meeting was my mentor Suzie Parkus. Her input was to make the membership page more functional & ready for immediate income.

As far as the franchise shows we are looking at Chicago in March & Houston in May. The London show wants $6000 to attend. Maybe down the road but definitely not now. Also considering a location in Brazil. I will make it happen this year.

Gearing up for Tony Robbins Business Mastery in West Palm Beach Been wanting to go to this for some time. Another dream becoming a reality.

> *Today I interviewed on my Podcast my Podcast coach Scott Doucet. He really believes in my mission. He has a clear understanding of what I'm trying to accomplish, and he complimented me on being a pioneer in my field.*

The loneliness of Entrepreneurs

I think that the general public and society at large, believe that the life of a business owner is fun and exciting, with little or no work. Well, this can be and often will be true, but the truth is that Entrepreneurs go days without sleep, work harder than anyone they know, and are very lonely.

When I am alone, that's when I can feel sad and start to think about things that have happened in my past. I don't let that stop me, I have too much work to do.

I have been in and out of relationships with men. Some of them created lifelong friendships, and others crashed and burned. I am working on my fear of being alone every day.

> *Entry: As my journey continues I find myself alone for many hours. I try so hard not to suffer in silence. It's that pain of loneliness I'm trying to master.*
>
> *Many men that come into my life want to either compete with me, hurry up & bed me, make me pay for everything, try to jump on my bandwagon of success or I'm just not attracted to them.*

I have faith someone will make the time to get to know me, that has his own thing going on with whom I am attracted to. So far this limbo stage is killing me. Not to mention all the time away from my family in Ohio.

My kids especially will never understand that mom is building an empire 1 brick @ a time for them.

Business Mastery

Today I write from the hotel awaiting the Tony Robbins Business Mastery I'm attending this week. I arrived in Palm Beach FL this morning & have a 3 hour zoom meeting with my Mentor & project manager Suzie Parkus from the UK.

A 3-hour meeting by the pool with her tech guy Simon Goodchild on board for about an hour... The cold hard facts laid out. I have a lot of people around me promising me the world & not delivering.

A meeting ending with me dismissing 4 team members upon my arrival back to NYC after TR.

Suzie is like my little Pitbull big sis taking charge & making everyone accountable.

My boy sending me 1 whole text seeing if I was ok. He had got drunk with his boy the night before & blew me off to recover. Blah blah blah. Another 1 about to bite the dust.

Met a friend during check-in whom I hung out with at the rest of TR's. We registered at TR then went for drinks after. Very nice shrink taking her biz to the next level. Well off to bed. Early gym call & Business Mastery take over :)

Day 1 Tony Robbins

Simply amazing & exhausting. Made 5 new girlfriends & a potential client husband/wife team for my membership. Saw a friend of mine Karim Ramos. Took several selfies lol.

Learned so much about the structure of my business. Time to hire more professional people & fire those who aren't delivering.

Tony Robbins and Sales Reps

Tony taught us that hiring 3 sales reps we can triple our revenue as long as they follow up.

We also heard from Keith Cunningham from TX who lost 100 million & made over 200 companies over 7 figures. He taught us accounting & that cash is not profits.

Spoke to my boy this morning. Think he may be the 1. Can't wait to see him again.

Business Financials with Tony Robbins

Another amazing day with Tony Robbins & Keith Cunningham. More on financials that I may be able to teach my boy a few things.

Made so many lifelong new friends & I even gave Tony Robbins a copy of my 1st book "Escape from the Darkness into the Enchanted" Got a picture of him holding it.

As I find myself exhausted I'm looking forward to hanging out with my new girlfriends after to relax. Once in a lifetime experience.

Return from Tony Robbins

Most energy backed conferences from leaders like Tony Robbins, end up leaving you depleted once you return home. Despite the energy high you get while there, you will experience a letdown and an emotional roller coaster.

While you are there, you absorb so much information, feel so elated, hell, almost HIGH from the energy, and let's be real – this is TONY ROBBINS! Knowing I would go through this sort of (Let Down), I was prepared to feel lonely again, as if something were missing, but I couldn't put my finger on it.

> My return from TR has been an emotional roller coaster. Before returning I contacted my friend who is like a young Tony Montana w/ whom I dated briefly & I asked him if he would pick up my cell from my assistant.
>
> She was great with the customers but not qualified to run the business. It was 5 months of pure hell. Repeating myself over & over to teach her the easiest of tasks.
>
> I had a full day of her & her much younger BF blowing up my phone with every slanderous thing they could think of. Once I told her she was returning my equipment or when I returned in the morning I would be reporting her to the police.
>
> I had to block her line & her BF from contacting me on several places including emails & social medias.

At least 1 of the girls I had met at BM was still in town for me to talk to about it. Miss Australia who's married to a big politician.

That night we met up with a huge paint contractor who asked if I would be his private pilot.

Back to NJ after Tony Robbins

Upon arriving back into NJ, the 1st day I just rested from my travels. The next day I put into actions firing my franchise guy who was making false promises & underdelivering. Also, my marketing expert I had to let go. That 1 I felt pretty bad about because he is a genuine nice guy. He just wasn't getting results.

So now I'm on this emotional downward spiral. So exhausting.

Today I had 2 podcast interviews. 1 with Jose Emilio Baez who was the 1st actor we hired with our company when it started to grow. He also placed 3rd in an Awesome Model Search in NJ which I was asked to be a judge at.

My next interview was with AJ Mihzrad. He is an amazing online coach & the reason I was able to Brand & create a membership site for KPC through his referral. He also set me up with a financial advisor who has helped me to double my money in a year.

Reflection

As I reflected on my business & personal life I realized I need to not let my kindness get in the way of business. The TR event also opened a whole slew of piloting jobs for me.

My main focus is getting my team up to par & get my piloting in full swing over the next 6 months, so I am able to attend TR BM 2 in Amsterdam or Netherlands.

Launch of Kids Party Characters Podcast

Today we launched Kids Party Characters Podcast on I-Tunes. I interviewed a mommy blogger yesterday Pollyanna Hale who helps mums with home workouts & has a healthy cookbook.

The launch was so exciting. I have people come up to me telling me they are listening in & they love it.

Please subscribe here:
http://bit.ly.KidsPartyCharactersPodcast

Meeting of the Minds with my Copilots

I just returned from the airport with a meeting with Jim Miller. He's an amazing helicopter pilot working for a charter company in Essex Airport. I met him hosting all his annual pilot parties.

Our meeting was about starting a flight club for all the corporates I met at TRBM event. He taught me about a company called Blade that is the helicopter Uber of Long Island. I'm going to approach some charter companies & make an offer after my website is finished. My new business venture underway.

About to make a new Podcast episode "The funniest moments at Kids Parties"

A New Sort of Relationship (Florida Bound)

One of my new friends asked me to come visit him in FL. That he would change his flight & book a hotel if I came. I arrive in Miami just in time to meet him for breakfast. We spent 2 beautiful days together.

He shared intimate details about his life & really opened up to me. The 1st night we went to a comedy club & had a lot of laughs. The next morning, we went to the gym. Me at Crunch & him on the bench.

After I worked out a flight at Tamiami airport where I got my twin Seminole hours at. We met a funny pilot who took him on his 1st flight ever. He loved it. He wants to start flying with me now.

The rest of the time in Miami I helped him to promote his book by making videos for Facebook. He ended by talking Skype with Carve with whom I connected him with.

They spoke highly of me to him. Tried to be supportive all along the way for him even though it wasn't so much fun for me. Where do we go from here? Only time will tell.

Life's Struggles

Here we go again the struggle of where my life is going. The pain of being alone building a business #10, a flight club. I know I can do this. I know people will talk. I know I will be creating more haters.

The men who can't handle a strong woman & the woman who think a woman's place is in the home making babies & keeping the house clean.

For some that works but for me I want more. I've always wanted more. I won't stop being me to make those who can't handle it happy. You can never make everyone happy.

Then there is the struggle wanting love in my life. Something real. A man who allows me to love them the way a woman should love a man.

A man who accepts me for who I am. Who doesn't try to change me or just use me in a sexual way.

A kind supportive hardworking man who takes care of himself the way I do myself. It's so hard to find. I struggle everyday what is the right thing to do.

Know my worth they say. Be patient they say. Trust the process they say. I'm left so confused to what is right or wrong. Who am I really? What do I really need?

The girls of BM

Then there's the girls of BM. A strong group of 5 woman I met at TR now having our 1st mastermind meeting via Zoom from Australia, to FL, to Canada to NYC with Kate holding us all accountable for our actions goals until our next meeting.

My 1st real biz partner

Who would have thought at a TR mastermind Meetup in NYC I would meet an amazing man? After the event a group of us went to a lounge for food & drinks.

He was hot as he sat across from me. Me trying not to stare. About 4 of us at the same table in deep conversations about business. What we all do for a living & an occasional inspirational quote to another.

He bought us a round of drinks. This was about a week before my book release party. So naturally I invited everyone at the table. They all showed too. As well as my actors, photographers & a couple of groupies too.

I also invited a friend I met on FB who owns a children's supplement drink. I interviewed him yesterday for my podcast.

I introduced this friend to the man from the meetup who owns an adult supplement drink co. That's my way of always trying to help people get to the next level.

Then there was the after party. My new friend drove me in his huge white truck. It should have had a latter that drops down when the door opens. That's how big.

Later that night I was on a 1st date with someone I met online.

My car was towed. At the tow shop who is behind me but this man I've been talking to for a few months now. We sporadically talked after that.

I saw online this Summit in NYC with some amazing speakers like Richard Branson & John Belford from the Wolf of Wallstreet. There he is again. I saw he had put something on FB about this event so while I was attending an Online Supercoach event in San Fran I bought a ticket to go hoping to run into him.

Both days we met for lunch or breakfast. Getting to know each other. A month goes by ad he texts me out of the blue. Now we start talking again. He had run into someone at TR Date with Destiny I referred him to. Both are now texting me they met.

He signed up for his book writing course & now he's publishing his book later that month.

Florida Bound Again...

I get this text to come meet (Mystery Man) in FL. Either come see him there or he would come see me when he gets back. Where's my credit card? Within 15 minutes of that text I'm sending him my itinerary & he's sending me the hotel info.

We talked about his bout with cancer and how he overcame it. Nice conversation but still not the relationship for me.

Telling me all about his childhood & how he had to be so tough. How his life was mostly on his own.

Found it all so endearing. Kind of afraid of this man but I know I have feelings for him. We talked about a new business venture I'm embarking on. He wants to be a part of it.

A girl that looks like me isn't always taken seriously so I need this man to be my Pitbull going into these meetings. The plan is put in motion.

Launching of his book

He's about to launch his book in 5 days so his coach asked him to do a 7-day video series building up to its release.

He had to show his vulnerable side. He referred to it as Tony Montana being vulnerable. All day he thought about what he was going to talk about then WHAM it hit him. We walked down the pier of Ocean Ave in Miami till he found a well-lit quiet spot. On a huge rock he made the most touching video it brought a tear to my eyes.

The next day our plan was to go flying. I had gotten my twin rating at Tamiami airport so the day before I made arrangements with the school. We arrived at the school & our instructor is the sweetest funniest 72-year-old pilot who breaks all barriers. He told us many stories of his years in aviation. Off we go into the sunset over Miami all 3 of us.

Me in the back filming it all.

Steep turns & stalls seem to be the thing to do to 1st time pilots. Of course, I knew it was coming but my friend did not. He loved it so much & all the way back to the hotel all he talked about was getting his license.

I said the same exact thing my 1st flight. That's why I became a pilot.

Back to NYC

I get to work on my flight club. A week goes by I text him about my progress on the project. He's in. My 1st real business partner possibly.

Another Let Down

Here we go. Another let down. Many times in life we have those who see how hard you work & want to just ride on your coat tails.

Where were you during the struggle? Don't mistake my kindness for weakness.

I'm very sensitive to those who only come around for what you can do for them. Keeping the faith that the right 1's will find their way into my life.

Live in the positive. A positive state influences your outcome. One must keep telling yourself to live there no matter what obstacles you get along the way.

Spread your wings it's time to fly. Make the leap own the sky.

Matter at Hand

Websites being built, 2nd & 3rd book underway, BF feeling closer. Now what?

As I'm having many conversations with Ireland, London & France franchise show experts I'm setting up booths for these shows. The feelings of this is somewhat surreal. How does a little corn-fed girl come to this point in my life?

The way I'm talking to these people about franchising like I know what I'm talking about when the truth of the matter is I know little but I'm learning along the way.

I find myself though talking the talk. Now it all comes down to money. Each of these shows are $3000-5000 to register plus all the paperwork, flights, airfare and rooms for my sales rep and actor.

Seems like a far-off vision slowly coming to fruition. I will make this happen. 1 brick at a time.

My goal is Houston in May, Ireland in September and London in February.

I met a franchise attorney at Tony Robbins who is helping with the paperwork.

Was going to TR so I could meet her or was it so I could stumble upon my newest business venture flight club or was it so I could get closer to the man of my dreams?

I'm not quite sure but I know in my heart and soul I'm on the verge of a breakthrough.

Flight Club

As I brainstorm in zoom meetings with my business partner and web developer we come up with a plan of attack. What we need to do to make this work. What we need to ask charter companies for. Now what do we call it?

I search the internet thesaurus putting in key words to name this company. I put a comment on social media's Facebook on my wall and in a group called **Coffee with Dan**.

I break the internet with over 400 comments come in with name suggestions. So fast I could hardly keep up with responding to them all.

Do they really want to help or are they just interested in the free flight I offered? Regardless of their intentions I was truly humbled by all the support.

It's interesting to see when you rise to the next level all the support you get from people just like you and all the hate from those who don't want you to advance.

I met my new man friend again for conversation and he suggest a Tapas/Wine bar in the middle of where we both live. The place is so loud we can't even think. He then suggests another place he knows of down the road. A quiet Italian type restaurant. In between brainstorming with title ideas for the flight club my friend talks about his childhood.

It took him six months to open up to me and I start to ask myself questions. Why is he doing this? Does he want to be my man? I know this for sure something is going on.

Needless to say, we still didn't figure out what to call this club. So, we agreed to meet again 2 nights later on.

Time to figure this out and to come up with copy to pitch to the charter companies.

What is Your Why

What is your "Why", your purpose, your beliefs, your cause. Why do you do what you do? Why should anyone care?

We all have our reasons. What drives us to do the things we do, what motivates us.

My grandbabies are mine. Being a teenage mother of 2 beautiful babies, struggling through college just trying to make ends meet is almost a mere memory. Something that made me the woman I am today.

Deep in your heart and soul is your why. Mine is so my grandbabies never have to endure the pain of living in poverty the way my kids had to.

My strength has taught my daughter the significance of self-reliance and hard work.

Now in my 40's I have my happy grandbabies which I must admit grandbabies are way better than kids. You can send them home after spoiling them.

So, find your Why. Whether it be so your kids never have to live in poverty, whether it be so you family can live a good life whatever that is to you or if being a positive force in society.

Now that you know a little more about how I faced the fire, started my businesses, turned my focus away from the dance clubs and bar scenes, as I detailed in my first book, it's time for you to make some life choices on your own. Whether it is about relationships or business, you must make choices.

Each choice starts a new path toward a new dream, and new goals. Each choice is yours to make, and the results are yours to own. In any relationship, ruffle some feathers and ask tough questions to avoid heartache.

Beyond the Enchanted is where the real work begins within yourself. So, "LET IT GO". Don't hold it in. Define your dreams, create the terms you want and rock this life.

Find your "Why" and hold onto it for dear life. My journey from the darkness to the Enchanted is about getting here, beyond the Enchanted and into a flow of life that fits by personality.

Currently I am building my membership site that is for teaching people the skills needed to start their own Kid's company franchise, as well as developing my own flight school training program and service.

THE INTERVIEWS

Meet My Heroes

Starting my podcast was a smart decision because it allowed me to truly perfect my elevator speech. In my first book, I go into the details of how I started by business, and how I spoke for the first time to a women's empowerment group; and was scared out of my wits! The podcast truly allowed me to connect with my audience at a deeper level than ever before.

Cheryl Jacobs:

Hi. Welcome to Kids Party Characters Podcast. I am dressed like Rapunzel. I just got done with a children's party right before this. Today, I would like to introduce a guest of mine. Mel Martin. He's been a mentor to me, and he's also an inspirational coach. And has become a true friend of mine. Hi Mel.

> **Mel Martin:** Hi. How are you? Happy New Year. Love, love, love the costume. I've never, ever had a conversation with Princess Rapunzel. This is the first, I'm totally honored to be here.

Cheryl Jacobs:

is actually our first conversation as me as a princess.

> **Mel Martin:** I know. It's totally awesome. I love it. Had you dressed like that walking around Times Square with me when I went to New York a couple months ago, I really would have been impressed. But no, this is fun. I love it.

Cheryl Jacobs:

In Times Square though, they probably would have thought I was one of those characters just getting money for $5.00 pictures.

> **Mel Martin:** I know right. You could have made a bunch, right?

Cheryl Jacobs:

Yeah. $5.00. I don't think ...

> **Mel Martin:** Five bucks. Anyway. Thank you for having me on. I'm really excited to be here, and I hope your year's off to a great start.

Cheryl Jacobs:

It is. Thank you. I actually met Mel through another inspirational coach, who runs onlinesupercoach.com website.. And the minute I met Mel, we instantly clicked.

> **Mel Martin:** Yes.

Cheryl Jacobs:

I went to a seminar that AJ Mihrzad was holding and sat by Mel. He invited me to sit next to him, he saved me a seat, and we acted like children. Little kids, trying to take the seminar seriously, but we pretty much just laughed the whole time.

> **Mel Martin:** Oh god. I've been to a lot of seminars, and you've got to create your own fun sometimes. Not to take anything away from AJ. I thought he was brilliant, and so were the other coaches. Brilliant enough to where, I'm a two-time speaker at that conference as well. It's something I take very, very seriously. I'm grateful for my relationship with AJ, because a lot of things have occurred since I met AJ, such as meeting someone like you. And I'm grateful for our friendship, and I love the fact that we collaborate, and we have a great friendship as well.

Cheryl Jacobs:

So, one of my questions is, where do you get all of your energy from? Because you always are so much ... so much energy. Every time I see you, and I'm like trying to take energy.

> **Mel Martin:** Like radiating, right? Like radioactive. That what it is? Am I glowing green? No, just kidding. You know, it's an interesting thing. Life has everything in it. And I am, at 53, I'm in awe of what I can do, and everything in my life that I get to do. And that's all by design and by choice. Taking all those lessons, all the painful ones, all the hard ones.

Everything. And just really deciding who I was going to be, and what action steps I was going to do. How I was going to be open and receptive to continue learning in the world and the universe and surrounding myself with just great people. Even the ones who aren't so great with their energy and learning from them and taking something away to either affirm or negate exactly what I want in my life, you know.

I have a life where I want for not. Okay. And I wake up to a wonderful, warm home that protects me. I have an incredible family. Physically, I'm in incredible athletic shape, 'cause I've taken care of myself. My inner circles, and the circles that I belong in are tremendous. There's nothing but gratitude that flows through me, because I allow life to flow through me. I don't let life happen to me … as much anymore.

Because we all have done that. I've addressed a lot of things in my life that I've kind of digested, and I feel all the feels, and I embrace everything, which is key. So, the energy that I have comes from an accumulation of all that. A total accumulation of all that. Spending time with you, getting to know you, being in contact with you. Seeing your growth and progression. Amazing. Amazing to me. That all lends to the energy that I have.

Because you have to decide if you're going to be a positive or negative asset to the universe, and you are just a form of energy.

Your embodiment in a physical sense, but at the end of it all, it's what you left behind, and how you were pivotal in that wheel of energy in the universe. It's a total choice. So, I choose to feel this way, and I absolutely just in love with the whole embodiment and process of it all. So, that's where it's from.

Cheryl Jacobs:

Well, I mean you definitely do these inspirational speeches all across the U.S. I know you've done New York. Have you done California, where you live?

> **Mel Martin:** Yes, I've had a blessed 34 year coaching career that is founded on strength and conditioning. I've coached, and worked and improved, and learned from post cancer patients all the way to major league ball players. And, I also was a top franchisee owner for Fitness Together, which was a personal training luxury franchise chain.
>
> And I was part of many panels for them. To ... As a panel expert speaking in front of a couple hundred owners, in annual retreats. I'm part of many groups like that. It's something I'm very comfortable with. It's something I really enjoy.
>
> I probably love doing it because ... There's a part of me, that if I can give somebody some insight and glimpse of what a journey could be like, from concept to action steps, to planning, to inception, to success, to road bumps, to loss, and then rebuilding.

If I can give them some sort of insight and glimpse to that and ... I'm gifted in the way I can articulate it, and I embrace that. Then I feel like I'm going to give something back to the universe, because it's blessed me with so many things.

Cheryl Jacobs:

And you currently work with Tim Matthews who I also see at AJ Mihrzad's seminar, and he's ... he created The Powerful Man, correct?

Mel Martin: Mm-hmm (affirmative) Yes, that program's been in ... existence for the last couple of years. I think about a year and a half or so. Tim Matthews is a brilliant, brilliant coach. He and I met, we were both on the speaking panel for the online super coaching conference this last April.

And he reached out to me, with the greatest compliment ever. There was a ... All the speakers, I believe there were 10 of us or so. Everybody got a 5 x 7 photograph of themselves with a big 11 x 14 frame.

And around it was just a white canvas where you could autograph it. The audience can autograph it. And you just get these unbelievable, heart warming messages from everybody, and compliments from everybody. And, honestly, it's a great kind of driving force to do those things, because of ... just for the fact that it makes you feel amazing, and appreciated.

Well, Tim wrote a little note on there saying, "Hey, love your energy. I'd love to have you join our team." It was very subtle. And, he specializes in The Powerful Man, which is an elite personal men's development program. And isolating the fact that men have a tendency to sacrifice themselves for their success, and not live with their most powerful self.

And, so we had a couple of conversations over the phone. And he's from the UK. I'm here in California. In Northern California. We had a couple of deep dives about it, just to see if it would fit. Then we decided, okay, let's start an onboarding process, and the easiest way for you to become a coach in anything, an educator, a leader in anything, is to be a student first.

I was a student in two programs that lasted eight weeks a piece. For sixteen weeks I was part of it, I graduated from it. The timing was critical. It was pivotal, because going through the program itself really shed a lot of light on my own life.

Which is what it had to do, otherwise I would not be able to coach at the level that they needed because it's a very intimate program. You're talking about men who are high achievers, who are not used to being vulnerable, who are not used to sharing their most deepest, intimate fears, in order to overcome them, in order for them to start completing and being whole.

I succeeded there, and I've been officially a coach with him, since this past November now. And it's amazing.

We work with small groups of six men. And between myself who's in California, I'm the lead coach here in North America. Tim handles the European market, 'cause he's in the UK. And then there's another American coach, from San Diego, he is now based in Taiwan in all places.

Between the three of us, we run this really an international, high level elite program, where we can work with four to six men from all over the world, who are high achievers, who fit that self-sacrifice model. And, we work with them twice a week through intense video conference calls with a lot of training and accountability throughout the week.

And within a six to seven, to maximum eight week period, we see some massive turn arounds. And they're now armed with some tools, and a system by which they can be, and live, and appreciate the powerful man within themselves.

We have a flagship program called The Inner Circle, where if you continue to invest in yourself, we are really going to take what you learned in the Active Vision method, which is what we call the initial program, for that first six to eight weeks, and then you really refine yourself. Because learning is remembering, and learning is application.

Once you learn it, now you gotta really apply it, right? So, that's what I do there. And I also own and I founded a program called FitLuvStrong. It's my own wellness program that I developed, it's effective wellness for those over 40, and also baby boomers, who want lasting results.

So, I've been developing that since my first introduction to AJ Mihrzad in October, actually August of 2016. I went to New York in October of 2016, I met him personally for the first time.

Cheryl Jacobs:

I think that was one week before I met you. It was right before.

Mel Martin: Yeah. Yeah. Absolutely. Became a student at his program then, and then he invited me back in April of last year, and in October of last year, to be a two time speaker, and I'm hoping he asks me back again this April, because my professional life and personal life have evolved from there. And coaching is a very intimate thing, and I applaud people who are called coaches, who ... such as yourself, myself, and others, who have the courage to step forward and say, "I have a voice, I have a message, and I think it could help you." But that in a nutshell is what I do professionally.

Cheryl Jacobs:

Yeah, I'm definitely new in this coaching business, and I have you, and I have AJ, and I have Tim Matthews to look up to, and a few others here and there. And, honestly, it's crazy 'cause I never even knew this business existed a year ago. And it wasn't until I met AJ, and you, and Tim, and some of the other speakers at the conference, that I even really decided to start this membership site, where I'm teaching everybody to own their own business, and coaching them through it, and all that. To be honest, I don't know where I would be today. I would still be ... I mean, I obviously still enjoy doing the kids' parties, but to teach people to own their own children's company is something that I would have never done without you guys.

I applaud you guys all for pushing me in the right direction, and thank you so much from the bottom of my heart for ... Especially you for helping me along the way personally, with my personal problems, and my business problems. You've always been there. And, so, I mean, and then you came to New York, we hung out. I took you to my best friend's gym.

> **Mel Martin:** That was awesome. That was brilliant. I gotta tell you.

Cheryl Jacobs:

And everything was awesome until you messed up my recording of my benching. You were like, "I got 25s on each side."

> **Mel Martin:** Oh well. "Yeah, can you do it again?"

Cheryl Jacobs:

I'm like, "Come on. No." Then five minutes later, I get this video of you working out, I'm like, "Thanks."

> Mel Martin: Talk about dropping the ball big time. No, it was funny. I'll never forget that moment, your ... I'm gonna do this. I look, "That's kind of impressive," right. I don't know what the hell happened, I don't know if I didn't press record or whatever.

Cheryl Jacobs:

You were just like, "Wow, she's really good."

> **Mel Martin**: Yeah. This is cool, yeah it's cool. I looked down, "Oh my god I didn't get that." I'm thinking, "It's just her first set, we'll do it again. And you're all, "No." I'm all ...

Cheryl Jacobs: Yeah, that was the last. Yeah, that was the heaviest set.

Mel Martin: "Oh. I didn't know that." I'm like, "Oh god, the moment of truth and I completely dropped it." But, you know, it's been an absolute pleasure getting to know you Cheryl. And I absolutely appreciate. And it's been ... it's been mutual. Thank you for acknowledging, or recognizing, and touching on the fact that I helped you. But, I gotta tell you, you helped me, and you've been a terrific friend, and just a real solid person in my life, considering the fact that I don't allow a whole lot of people in my life, and I think as you become more refined, and more successful, and hard working in your life, you really understand the value of your emotional energy, and time. So, I surround myself with top notch people, and I consider you as one of those. I ...

Cheryl Jacobs: Thank you.

Mel Martin: Very welcome. Yeah. It's ... It's one of those things where ... Becoming a coach is almost like the next level because in what you do, and what I was doing as well, you have to expand from a local and regional level if you want to reach that next level. And the internet has allowed our worlds to shrink, because there is not enough customer pool locally where you're at, for you to grow at the level you want to grow. The next step is to coach somebody, and teach somebody the working model that works for you. If you wanna do true replication, that's where it's at. Being a multi-site, or a multi-business coach, owner, is the next step. You don't have a brick and mortar business where you set up shop, and people go there and they hire you, and you're paying lease rent on a space, right? It's a different kind of a service.

If that were the case though, that means you'd have to be a multi-location owner regionally where you're at. Starting regionally. That's difficult to do because you've got a lot of liabilities there. The rent, the liability insurance, employees, pay roll. That mounts up. In the online coaching world, you have none of that. None. And it's a brilliant model. And in your case, teaching people how to become franchisee owners in the same model that's been very successful for you, especially on a market where it's not ever going to run out, ever. As long as children are being born, and as long as Disney is making movies, you've got job security. You've got absolute enterprising security. I absolutely love what you're doing.

Cheryl Jacobs:

I just want to touch on that. The crazy thing about my business is, there's a child born every day. And I've seen people ... I've done parties from where they have five princesses, it's catered, they have 100 guests, five princesses come in, and I've done it in not so nice areas of the Bronx, or in Brooklyn. But, let me tell you something, people will spend money on their children's parties before they'll pay their rent, if they have to.

And that's the crazy thing about this business, is there's children's birthdays every single day, and it's not a saturated market, that's why I really wanted to help people to take what I've learned to give to you, because it's a business where it brings so much happiness to people, so much happiness to children. If I could do it for free, and I didn't have to make a living, I would do it. That's why I want to share this with everyone.

> **Mel Martin:** Well, luckily you don't have to do it for free. There's a value to it. And ... when you were first sharing this with me, I thought to myself, "Wow, what a great national reach." And then, you went to the UK, and you said the words, "I have a franchisee that might happen in the UK." And I thought to myself, of course. Of course. Why not. There's Euro Disney. Hell, there's Disney in China, there's Disney in Japan. It's an international reach. Kudos to you. Absolutely.

Cheryl Jacobs:

I actually dressed like Elsa and took photos by the London tower, which I will show people soon here. And, you know, the minute the children saw me, there was ... they had to be like, not nursery students. Like new nursery children, three, four years old. And the minute they saw me, their mouths just dropped. So, I know there's a huge market there, and no one's doing it.

> **Mel Martin:** Well, you're real. You're real to them. Right? All of the sudden.

Cheryl Jacobs:

Yeah, they still believe.

> **Mel Martin:** Yeah. There's this cartoon character on the screen, or on DVD, or on Netflix, and all of the sudden she's walking around London.

Cheryl Jacobs:

By the Tower Bridge, taking photos.

> **Mel Martin:** How awesome. "Mommy, it's Elsa. Look, I want her for my party." I mean, come on, you know what I mean? Yeah, right? "Can she come over?" You know, all that.

Cheryl Jacobs:

I think you need to work on your British accent.

> **Mel Martin**: I know it sucks, but you know what, I lived in London for as ... Oh, yeah, I love that. See. Awesome.

Cheryl Jacobs:

That's my Facebook page, by the London Bridge is Elsa.

> **Mel Martin:** I was jealous when you went to the UK, 'cause I lived in the UK for about six months. I spent a semester there for about six months. I lived in Kensington gardens, and I went to ULU, University of London. And I love the British culture. I love British films. So, when you went, I was all like, "Oh. I wanna go." But you know what,

Cheryl Jacobs:

I love it there. I absolutely love it there.

> **Mel Martin:** Right. I'm going in 2018. At some point this year. I keep saying 2018 as if it's still 2017. I'm going this year. Sometimes I would guess between now ... sometime between May to August. Tim is going to decide if we're going to do a large event, couple of hundred people, couple of hundred men, in a seminar. In a Tony Robbins type seminar. Or, we're going to do small group retreats. Mountain side retreats. Spiritual retreats. He's done a couple. The last one he did was Himalayas, and the last one prior to that was in the French Alps. I am pumped for that. I am going to be leading one of those. I'm going to be speaking in one of those. I'm really, really excited about that.

Cheryl Jacobs:

Yeah? Well, my UK London franchise opens in March. So, maybe I could come back and help my franchisee, just use that as my excuse to come say hello to you and Tim.

> **Mel Martin:** Yes. Absolutely. You kidding? That's awesome. I don't know. What else? What else is going on?

Cheryl Jacobs:

There's nothing else. Well, I mean, we just started this, you are actually our first interview, I'm so happy that I'm able to get you on, because I know that your schedule is crazy, and mine's crazy, and we can finally hook it up. Even our lighting and our sound is good. So happy about all of that.

> **Mel Martin:** Are you kidding? I'm using my brand new iPhone X, and it looks brilliant, so I'm very, very happy.

Cheryl Jacobs:

And, you know, you requested that I not change after my kids' party, so here I am.

> **Mel Martin:** I know. Right. You're like, "I'm gonna be." And, "Do I get to see you in your costume?" You're all like, "No. I'm gonna get out of the clothes." I'm like, "Oh. What?"

Cheryl Jacobs:

So, just for you, I decided to stay in costume.

> **Mel Martin:** Yay. Oh my god.

Cheryl Jacobs:

All right. So, I just, just let me wrap this up, and I'm going to ... What is your Facebook page again?

Mel Martin: Just simple. Mel Martin. Just look me up under Mel Martin. Everything is there. I record ... geez, in three years, I've done about close to 300 Facebook Live and video recordings. And I touch on a variety of topics. There are three essential things that I believe that are solid in a maximum wellness program which is, strengthen your body, and strengthen your heart and mind, and make sure you feed yourself properly. As basic as that sounds, it's a lot more to it than that. I'm in the process of finalizing and refining a six week, "Your Health is Your Wealth" system that I'll be releasing really, really soon. I'd love to share it with you, and the world. And, I'd love to learn from all of you.

I'm in a pay it forward business, meaning that my professional biography, and every person that I've helped in the last 34 years, taught me to be the coach that I am, so that together, with all those people in the past, we all help the person that I work with now, and in the future. I'd love to learn from you. You can always private message me on Facebook. You can look me up on Instagram @FitLuvStrong. Capital F-I-T, capital, L-U-V, capital S-T-R-O-N-G. And you can message me there as well. So, anything you're going through, or whatever, any question you may have, if I can, I'll help you with it. And if not, at the least, I'll learn from you, and take it from there.

Cheryl Jacobs:

Awesome, well thank you Mel for being on the show.

Mel Martin: Oh, you're very welcome.

Cheryl Jacobs:

I'm sure I'll talk to you soon.

> **Mel Martin:** Yeah. My pleasure. And I'd love to come on again if there's any time. All right?

Cheryl Jacobs:

Sounds good.

> **Mel Martin:** Okay.

Cheryl Jacobs:

Have a good day.

> **Mel Martin:** Thanks Cheryl, take care. Bye bye.

Cheryl Jacobs:

You're welcome. Bye.

Podcast Guest AJ Mihrzad

Cheryl Jacobs:

Hi, I'm Cheryl Jacobs and welcome to Kids Party Characters Podcast. Thanks for listening, make sure you subscribe below. Today, I'd like to welcome AJ Mihrzad. He is the author of "Mind Body Solution: Train Your Body for Permanent Weight Loss." He's also appeared on Entrepreneur Magazine and "How to Grow Your Coaching Business to Over a Million Dollars a Year." He is the owner of Online Super Coach Podcast and also onlinesupercoach.com. He's probably one of the most influential super coaches and speaker and the man behind massively marketing Kids Party Characters Company and the importance of bringing value to others before yourself. Hi, AJ.

> AJ Mihrzad: Hey, Cheryl. Thanks for having me. This is such an amazing thing to be on your podcast. Just a year ago, we were talking about podcasts and now you have your own, so what a celebration.

Cheryl Jacobs:

Yeah. I honestly didn't even know that there was podcasts, other than DJs, until I met you. When you told me that, I was like, "Wow, you have your own podcast." I was so amazed. Okay, let's talk about a year ago when I met you.

Probably a little over a year ago I met you, and you taught me about the world of Online Super Coach, which I knew nothing about because I was more posting selfies probably and my modeling pictures on Facebook and not really using it as a tool for marketing or a business or anything like that. You taught me all about that and most likely the reason why I went on to turn my company into a membership site. Tell people about how you bring out their super powers.

> **AJ Mihrzad:** Yeah, definitely. It's very impressive. You definitely are the selfie queen. I love how you transitioned from being a selfie queen to marketing yourself and branding yourself on social media, which is going to make you a lot more money. Cheers to that. I always ask people, "Do you want to be rich or do you want to be famous?" I think a lot of times people just want to be famous on social media, but you can really monetize your brand, your business, your career using social media. Let's talk about that.

Cheryl Jacobs:

Yeah, social media and good copy. I actually just studied copyrighting and infotainment, which is another thing that you taught me about, so I went into that and studied that. That's a huge thing for marketing here. You do seminars all over New York and I'm sure I know saw you in San Francisco as well. Anywhere else that you've done seminars?

AJ Mihrzad: Yeah, at my house. I started doing seminars at my house. I had 40 women in my living room last weekend for the Female Entrepreneur Seminar. That was a lot of fun. Now I could do them at my house. I'm going to LA actually in two days to do a seminar there. Now I'm taking it nationwide.

Cheryl Jacobs:

Yeah, I saw that you had all those chairs in your living room for all those women. When you put something on there that you were going to have 40 women in there, I'm like, "Hmm, now where is he going to put all these women?" I know your living room's large, but still they're growing. The very first one I think you did, there was probably half that number of women.

AJ Mihrzad: Yeah, it was about 25.

Cheryl Jacobs:

Yeah, and you were okay with the couches and the chairs then, but then I was like, "Okay, he's just doubled his size. How is he going to do this?"

AJ Mihrzad: Yeah. I think that's a big part of entrepreneurship and something I've seen you done really well is jumping off a cliff and then building wings on the way down. It's committing to certain things, not knowing the how, knowing what you want to do, why you want to do it, and then everything just falls into place, just like your amazing company. It's grown tremendously in the past year. You've now really invested in yourself, taking your whole life to the next level. You're making a bigger impact, helping so many more people. It's like you had that vision a year ago and then you took the appropriate actions. I'm really proud of you for that.

Cheryl Jacobs:

Yeah, thank you. Yeah, no more selfies, it's all about branding Kids Party Characters right now.

AJ Mihrzad: Yes.

Cheryl Jacobs:

A few selfies along the way.

AJ Mihrzad: Yeah, here and there.

Cheryl Jacobs:

I know. It's weird, because on Facebook, it comes up, like, five years ago, what you did, and I got my modeling pictures or the selfies. Thank God the club pictures aren't coming up anymore. It's like you look at where you've been and to where you are now. If you do the right thing by yourself in your company, it's amazing transformation that you do. Okay, we talked about the female entrepreneurs. I saw you speaking to the children. What was that about? I briefly saw it on Facebook.

> **AJ Mihrzad:** Oh, yeah. The whole thing is, many people don't know this, but prior to me starting my business, I taught health and physical education. I was a teacher for about three years. That's what made me realize two things, one, I love teaching people, I love educating them, and two, after working with kids for three years, I prefer working with adults. Kids are cool, but-

Cheryl Jacobs:

See, we're opposite.

> **AJ Mihrzad:** Yeah. They're a little less motivated than an adult. I feel like I could do more with adults, you know what I mean? Kids, they're pretty limited. They can't start a business. They can't get a six-pack.

Cheryl Jacobs: Although, I've seen some little kids with six-packs. It's pretty crazy. They're lifting with their fathers and stuff like that.

> **AJ Mihrzad:** Yeah. You ever put a kid on a strict diet? Kids can't go on low carb.

Cheryl Jacobs:

Low carb and no candy. Yeah, that would not work. The good thing about my business is that I'm there to entertain them and you're there to try and teach them nutrition, which I think, maybe focusing on a little bit older, like maybe teens, because younger kids, they don't want to cut out candy and cake and stay focused on, other than playing with the other kids.

> **AJ Mihrzad**: It's hard to get a kid to wake up every morning at 5:00 a.m. and do an hour of cardio.

Cheryl Jacobs:

That would be really funny. Although, I have seen some kids do videos where they're lifting and stuff like that and they're so little. It's funny.

> AJ Mihrzad: Yeah, it's cute.

Cheryl Jacobs:

That's like a one in a million, though.

> **AJ Mihrzad:** Yeah. No, but I do love kids. I have a lot of respect for them. I was a kid not too long ago, so I connect with them.

Cheryl Jacobs:

You have a little niece, too, right? Let's talk about when I first met you. I think that's how I met you, because I was like, "He's got a daughter and he might like my kids parties." That's why I was like, "Hey, your daughter is beautiful." That's how we actually met on Facebook. She's how old now?

> **AJ Mihrzad:** She's going to be three in two weeks.

Cheryl Jacobs:

Oh, wow.

> **AJ Mihrzad:** Yeah.

Cheryl Jacobs:

If I were to send one of my girls over to entertain for her third birthday, what do you think she would like?

> **AJ Mihrzad:** That is a great question. I don't know her cartoon-watching habits. I remember, because I'm the oldest of four boys, I have three younger brothers, and I would always see them watching kid's television and stuff like that. My little brother was really into Barney, the purple dinosaur. Is he still relevant?

Cheryl Jacobs:

You know what? When I first started my company and I first got asked by the agent, first it was, "Will you play Cinderella?" Then, the second one was, "Will you play Barney?" It's not as fun as the princesses, but he rarely gets booked. Honestly, really funny story is I lived in New York City. You don't need a car in New York City.

Here I am on the subway with this garbage bag of Barney and looking like a homeless person, carrying this thing on the subway and the bus over. I had to go to the Staten Island, so I had to do the ferry on top of it with this huge garbage bag. Barney's not so fun, but he doesn't really get booked so much anymore.

> **AJ Mihrzad:** Yeah, I guess it's the '90s, right? Yeah, you know what? That's a great question. I'll ask her next time to see what she's into.

Cheryl Jacobs:

Yeah.

> **AJ Mihrzad:** You told me a really interesting fact and, to this day, I'm fascinated by it. You said there's a certain age where kids could tell between what's real and what's imaginary. Once you have them in that imaginary phase, they believe that they're with Barney or with the girl from Frozen and all this stuff, Elsa, yes.

Cheryl Jacobs:

Elsa. Yes, that's Elsa or Anna.

> **AJ Mihrzad:** What is the age where kids know that it's fake?

Cheryl Jacobs:

I would say up until eight. They still believe up until they're eight. When they're seven, there's a couple that are questionable, but up until eight. I mean, I've done parties for 10-year-olds before and they still believe.

> **AJ Mihrzad:** Wow, slow learners.

Cheryl Jacobs:

Slow learners or maybe their mom and dad are protecting them, I don't know. I would say eight is pretty much the cutoff. For your niece, for three, she's at that age where it's either a mascot, like maybe Paw Patrol is big right now or PJ Masks is big right now. Mickey and Minnie is always popular, but she also could go with the princesses or superheroes, too. She's right at that kind of transitional age right there.

> **AJ Mihrzad:** How do you stay up on the trends and know what the little kids like?

Cheryl Jacobs:

Well, obviously I have two grandbabies, two and five. They always tell me what they like. I mean, their toys, I have millions of toys. Plus, the parents, when they call, what's requested the most and things like that.

I actually just got a call today, there's a new moving coming out for a new princess and I have to look into. Right now, emojis is starting to get requested. I don't know if I want the poop emoji.

AJ Mihrzad: Yikes.

Cheryl Jacobs:

I have a feeling it's going to be requested, so I might look into that one.

AJ Mihrzad: Yeah. It sounds like a great birthday party.

Cheryl Jacobs:

I know. Well, they asked me to face paint that on their face and I'm like, "Okay, no problem, if that's what you want."

AJ Mihrzad: Wow, okay. Kids these days.

Cheryl Jacobs:

Or the hearts, they want the hearts on the eyes, like the hearts emoji, you know? The one on their eyes and the smiley face. I do that one a lot.

AJ Mihrzad: Yeah, the younger generation is interesting, especially nowadays. Did you hear about the Tide Pod Challenge, that the kids are eating Tide Pods?

Cheryl Jacobs:

I don't even know what a Tide Pod is. What is that?

AJ Mihrzad: Basically, when you do your laundry, instead of pouring detergent, they have these pods called Tide Pods.

Cheryl Jacobs:

Oh, yeah. Okay.

> **AJ Mihrzad:** They're basically pods that explode when you do the laundry. There's this phenomenon now, it's a hashtag, The Tide Pod Challenge, and there's a lot of little kids, even teenagers, that basically eat the Tide Pods. They film themselves biting into it, so it explodes in their mouth and actually a few cases of death.

Cheryl Jacobs:

I'm sure.

> **AJ Mihrzad:** There were, I think, five kids who died and three adults who died. They ate the Tide Pods. If you look for the hashtag, you'll see them on pizzas and they have Tide Pod sandwiches. It's a new trend that people eat them, they videotape themselves on social media. I was like, "That's really interesting how in different eras, in the '80s and '90s, kids were into different things." Now, it's eating detergent.

Cheryl Jacobs:

I think that's like sniffing glue. When I was a kid, that was the thing to do. I could see the kids doing stupid things like that, but-

> **AJ Mihrzad:** At least when you sniff glue, you get high. You get a benefit. This is like you're just eating the chemicals.

Cheryl Jacobs:

That's insane, and then adults are doing it?

AJ Mihrzad: There's nothing glamorous about that.

Cheryl Jacobs:

That's retarded. I don't understand why adults would do that, too. Are you serious? I could see kids doing that.

AJ Mihrzad: Yeah, adults that died from it. That's living life on the edge, definitely.

Cheryl Jacobs:

Obviously, I have to thank you for pushing me. You connected me up with a brand name company that created the membership site.

AJ Mihrzad: Thank you, yes.

Cheryl Jacobs:

Without you, I totally put my focus and now we have this membership site.

For anybody that's interested, for stay-at-home moms or anybody who's looking for a second business, you can run it through your home. You can start off the first year making six figures and grow it from there. Another thing, too, you inspired me to write my first book.

AJ Mihrzad: Yes.

Cheryl Jacobs:

It's "Escape From the Darkness"-

AJ Mihrzad: Journey Into the Enchanted, yes.

Cheryl Jacobs:

It's "Escape From the Darkness Into the Enchanted."

AJ Mihrzad: That's powerful. Yeah, your autobiography.

Cheryl Jacobs:

Autobiography from a teenage mother to owning my ninth business, kidspartycharacters.com. It's a bestseller on Amazon right now, still is. I think we launched it in August. Yeah, launched it in August, still a bestseller. Thank you for the five-star review.

AJ Mihrzad: Yeah, it's a phenomenal book. I'm proud of you. So many people say they're going to write a book and you actually do it. It's amazing to see how far you've come. When we first met a little over a year ago, you just had your company. Now, you have this amazing membership portal and you built this international following, all these people on social media, it's amazing.

You're doing a great thing, because essentially that's what I do. I have a company called Online Super Coach and I help personal trainers and coaches to grow their online business. They basically buy my courses or come to my seminars to get the shortcut. It took you so many years to learn all the things that you did and now you give them a shortcut so that they could start the business literally next weekend.

Cheryl Jacobs:

Yeah. The reason I did that is to help them, because all the mistakes that I made when I first started. There were companies out there that have beautiful pictures of Mickey Mouse and they probably stole it from Disneyland or something like that. Then, I get it and it's scary Mickey. I'm like, "I can't send this to a kid's party, because who's going to call me back when they are going to be like, 'Oh, these costumes are bootleg or something'?" I eliminate all the mistakes, who's the good advertisers. I have a casting director on staff right now so that you can get talent.

AJ Mihrzad: Backpage is a prostitution magazine.

Cheryl Jacobs:

Yeah, completely different.

AJ Mihrzad: Like, escorts.

Cheryl Jacobs:

Backstage is for actors, Backpage is for hookers.

AJ Mihrzad: Yes.

Cheryl Jacobs:

It's completely different. Yeah, I eliminate all the guesswork. I basically give them the platform from beginning to up and running. I sold my first membership. I just attended Business Mastery, so I sold my first membership.

AJ Mihrzad: Shout out to Tony Robbins, yes.

Cheryl Jacobs:

Yes, first membership to a husband/wife team. She's a stay-at-home mom and he's the bread-earner. She's like, "I need to make more money," because they want to go on vacations. I'm like, "Guess what I have for you?" She has children, so it's perfect. She works well with children already, so it's first membership sold. I'm looking forward to that. We're opening up a franchise in London this March, so that's our first global Kids Party Characters.

AJ Mihrzad: Congratulations. That's huge, going international.

Cheryl Jacobs:

Yes. You have a new book coming out, too, right? Don't you have another book that you're writing right now, your second?

AJ Mihrzad: Yes. It's in the process of being written, but yeah. It's more of like a philosophy book just on mindset. One thing I'm really into, I have a master's in psychology, is I do a lot of research on what creates the fastest change in someone? I've come to find it's the power of identity. How you perceive yourself equals your success or your failure in life. When you think, act and speak like a certain person, you soon become that person.

Cheryl Jacobs:

Yeah. Fake it until you make it, that's not really what you're saying?

AJ Mihrzad: Not really fake it until you make it, more like act as if and soon you will become.

Cheryl Jacobs:

There you go. I like that better.

> **AJ Mihrzad**: Yeah. It's like becoming that person mentally and then taking the actions. For example, someone wants to become a millionaire. The fastest way to become the millionaire is if they ask themselves, "Who do I have to be in order to deserve a million dollars? What do I do on a daily basis? How can I serve a million people?" Then, soon you become that, so how does a millionaire think, how do they speak, how do they act. When you have that identity, you become that person.

Cheryl Jacobs:

Yeah. I think that's why your push to brand my company and the membership, I was in my little bubble of New York, New Jersey, Connecticut only. My families from Ohio, so we started a franchise over there. Well, not really a franchise, it's a territory. We're calling it "territories," not franchises, but from when I went to London and now we're opening up in Chicago as well and then the husband and wife team from Tony Robbins. That, I think getting out of my bubble and out of my own way is basically what you're teaching, to basically get out of your own way, to get your mindset of, "Okay, I can take this business bigger and make it bigger." You just got to put your mind to it and do it.

AJ Mihrzad: Yeah. I have a lot of different courses and programs. Just two weekends ago, I had a course on helping people write a book in two days. I had 12 people come to my house and we had a whole process of getting the book out of them and setting up the title and the whole outline of the book, publishing it, making it a bestseller, just like you. Those are people that took action. You took action.

There's so many people that say, "I want to write a book. I want to start a business. I want to make all these changes," but they talk about it and they never do it. A few people that actually do it, they're the action-takers. It's like you already have a vision of what you want to do and now it's getting out of your own way and actually executing on it.

Cheryl Jacobs:

Yeah. I never saw you put anything on Facebook. I'm a follower on Facebook of you, but I didn't see it. When I saw my friend, D, introduced you guys, I was like, "You got meet AJ. You guys would be good together." I knew it the minute you guys met. You're both texting me from Date with Destiny. You're both texting me, like, "Cheryl, I met D." "I met AJ." It was crazy. You were like, "He signed up for my book event." I was like, "He's been saying he wanted to do that for a while." I'm so glad you guys met and got that together.

AJ Mihrzad: Yeah, thank you for the connection.

Cheryl Jacobs:

Yeah, and now his book is coming out soon here, I believe.

AJ Mihrzad: Next month, yeah.

Cheryl Jacobs:

Next month, that's awesome.

> **AJ Mihrzad:** Yeah. D's a great guy. He's an action-taker. I met him at a Tony Robbins seminar. Within five minutes of meeting, he gives me his credit card. He was like, "I want to buy it. I don't care how much it costs. Sign me up." I'm like, "Okay, this guy is serious." He came to my book event and wrote his book in two days. It was a really powerful story of surviving leukemia, becoming this "troubleshooter," as he calls it.
>
> Then, after that, he signed up for my online coaching program to take his online business to the next level. Again, I love working with people like D, people like you. It's like you guys just do it, right? You don't talk about it, you get it done. Action-takers, they make the world go around.

Cheryl Jacobs: Yeah, definitely. I saw his post today. I was so happy. How many other people were at your book event? A few, right?

> **AJ Mihrzad:** 12 in total. Yes, 12 people.

Cheryl Jacobs:

That's awesome. They all have their books coming out in about a month, right?

> **AJ Mihrzad:** Yes. Yeah, I set up a specific launch date. Everyone's launching at a different week, so like February, March, April. It's awesome, because prior to working with them, I helped 20 people become authors. I did it through my online program, virtual students, coaching students. This is the first time that I was able to get 12 authors in one room together and, over the course of a weekend, get their books out. It's actually something I'm going to be doing more often, just based on how great this event went. A lot of people say, "Hey, I want to do the next one," so maybe every few months I'll run a book retreat out of my house.

Cheryl Jacobs:

Well, it's a great thing, because nobody's doing it, for one. You're the first person I've ever seen do it. When I wrote my book, I found a ghostwriter to help me through it. You need a coach, for one, to get out of your way. There's a process that people don't understand. I had over a hundred pages, which my book was narrowed down to 60, because she put it in story format. Without her, I couldn't have done that. You connected them up with the right people and now, look-it, now you have a total of 32 people that you've helped with their books.

AJ Mihrzad: Yeah, it's the best feeling. I think that's the cool thing about what you do and what I do. You not only make a great living out of it, but also it's very fulfilling. When you see the smiles on the kids' faces and people are just generally happy with the process, it feels really good. If you're, I don't know, I'm thinking about other jobs, a retail store or an accountant, you're not really transforming lives on a daily basis. It's cool when you could make money, but at the same time fulfill other people's lives.

Cheryl Jacobs:

Yeah. This business, the kids company, when I started, I'm more behind the scenes now, but when you go into a kid's party and you see how happy they are and you see how happy their parents are to see their kids happy, I would do it for free if I didn't have to make a living. I've done a lot of charity events. The mothers will tell me, "This is the first time my daughter has smiled in a month," because I do a lot of hospitals and children with autism and stuff like that. It always makes me cry. I don't know why, I can never keep it back. The mom starts crying and I'm like, "Stop crying, because you're going to make Cinderella cry."

It really is, to bring happiness to other people is probably the biggest reason why I started the membership site. Instead of just keep it in this little area, why not bring it across? Even when I went to Brazil and everybody knows who Elsa and Spiderman is over there and all these characters. When I went to London, I dressed like Elsa and did a photo shoot by the Tower Bridge. There was a little nursery school of children there and their mouths just dropped when they saw Elsa.

>**AJ Mihrzad:** Wow.

Cheryl Jacobs:

Yeah. I know there's a market for this everywhere. I've done both ends of the spectrum, where people will have five characters for a one-year-old, catered, and a DJ and everything else. Then, I've gone to not-so-nice areas in the Bronx or Brooklyn or something like that and you know that they haven't paid their rent that month, but they'll have two princesses there and make their children's birthday special. People, they just want to make their kids happy. It's such a fulfilling thing. I've found my passion.

>**AJ Mihrzad:** Yeah, I love it. No, I could hear it in your voice, you're really living your life's purpose.

Cheryl Jacobs:

Yeah. What's next with you? I haven't spoken to you in a while. What else are you doing with yourself over there?

AJ Mihrzad: Well, I set a big goal in 2017 to do my first night of standup comedy. I'm happy to say that I was able to accomplish it October 6th of 2017. It was the biggest joy of my life, because I've always wanted to do standup. Not so much as a career, but because I do seminars and a lot of public speaking, I've always challenged my communication. I stuttered for the first 20 years of my life and I always had a fear of public speaking. By doing my own seminars and stepping out of my comfort zone, I always become better.

I kind of felt like standup comedy was my big challenge in terms of getting up there, telling jokes, being vulnerable. When you do standup, if you suck, people heckle you or they make fun of you. They throw tomatoes at you. If you're public speaking, even if you suck, they'll just clap and be like, "Good job." I knew I had to challenge myself.

Cheryl Jacobs:

Is this going to be your thing? Are you going to keep doing it?

AJ Mihrzad: Yeah, I'm doing more standup comedy, definitely, and adding more infotainment to my seminars and my videos. I set a big goal for this year. I cringe, I get scared when I talk about it, but it's to record a rap album. That's my-

Cheryl Jacobs:

That's your new challenge?

AJ Mihrzad: That's my new challenge. I love hip-hop music. I've always been fascinated with rappers who could rhyme for 20, 30 minutes at a time. Then, I started to practice freestyling. I started practicing 10, 20 minutes a day and I realized, the more I did it, the better I got. I could just flow and just freestyle. Then, I said, "If I become better at freestyle, then I could speak better. I could be more on the fly, more spontaneous, improvisational."

Then, I said, "Well, if I record a rap album, who I become in that process will be a better communicator." I'm not doing it to win a Grammy. I'm not doing it to make money off the album itself, but I want to inspire people, teach them lessons and also take my content and teach it through music. I love teaching. Instead of just speaking or telling jokes, now I could create an album and people could learn from my musical talent.

Cheryl Jacobs:

That's a great idea, to have people, infotainment, to rap. I don't think anybody's doing that either, so you'll be a pioneer.

    AJ Mihrzad: I would love to see a Kids Party Characters rap album.

Cheryl Jacobs:

The intro to something.

    AJ Mihrzad: Yeah. I could see you being a really good rapper, if you ever wanted to pursue that.

Cheryl Jacobs:

I know I'm good at singing "Let it Go," and all that kind of stuff, those princesses' songs, but I'm not sure about rapping.

> **AJ Mihrzad**: Give it a try. You were in the nightclub scene, right? What genre of music? You could probably DJ. You could create something.

Cheryl Jacobs:

Yeah. It would have to be with house music. I'm a house person. I like house music.

> **AJ Mihrzad:** No, exactly. You could sing a house song, "Let it Go," the house music version.

Cheryl Jacobs:

The house music rap version.

> **AJ Mihrzad:** Exactly.

Cheryl Jacobs:

That would be hilarious. Oh, my goodness. I know there was another question that I wanted to, I don't remember what it is right now. Oh, your video with the car coming in the driveway, what was that about?

AJ Mihrzad: Yeah. I went through a whole rebranding process and I hired this team to help me with my videos, my website, my marketing, all that stuff. They're really talented guys and they created this trailer, this video commercial of what I do. The biggest thing that I teach people is to create their ideal lifestyle. That's one of the reasons why I have so many events in my house. I live in a beautiful house, it's a nice mansion. There's a lot of open space. Six months ago, I purchased my dream car, which is a Bentley Convertible. They had this whole idea of showing the lifestyle, the car, the house, the luxury. Then, I'm teaching content while they're filming these.

It was an experiment. It actually worked really well. Oddly enough, my business has grown significantly once I showed them my lifestyle. I'm teaching people how to grow their online business and how to become financially independent. I live by example. I'm really grateful to create a lot of financial abundance, so I'm like, "You could learn from my example."

My students, they do well for themselves as well. In fact, the other day, one of my students from Australia, made his first million dollars. He broke seven figures in his business. We've been coaching together, and he shared a screenshot, "I just broke a million dollars." I took a screenshot of that, post it on my Facebook with a little backstory of him breaking a million dollars in this business.

That really makes me happy, because it's like I just don't like to teach people, I also want to show results. That's why I always tell people, "Don't give me your advice, show me your results." People that show the results of what they do, they don't really have to talk that much. It's showing and not telling.

Cheryl Jacobs:

Yeah, I agree. I, since I got back from Business Mastery, reevaluated my team. The people that weren't showing results are no longer with me. The ones that are doing amazing, I'm giving them raises. You really have to reevaluate everything about people and what their results are.

> **AJ Mihrzad:** Well, the question is, when are you going to buy your dream car?

Cheryl Jacobs:

When I have a garage to park it in or unless I'm going to come over and park it in your garage. You have space for, how many, 10 cars or something like that?

> **AJ Mihrzad:** Yeah, I got a lot of space. Yeah, you can park it here. I'll drive it on the weekends.

Cheryl Jacobs:

As long as it's not snowing outside.

AJ Mihrzad: Yes. We know that. What would be your dream car, though, if you could have any car on the planet?

Cheryl Jacobs:

I'm not really sure, because I've never really grew up with luxury cars.

AJ Mihrzad: Me neither. I was very poor.

Cheryl Jacobs:

Yeah. I would have to really investigate to look into it.

AJ Mihrzad: I see you in a pink Lamborghini.

Cheryl Jacobs:

No, I'm not a pink person. I'm more of a tomboy, so it would probably be more something-

AJ Mihrzad: Black Lamborghini.

Cheryl Jacobs:

Maybe black or gray. Maybe dark gray.

AJ Mihrzad: Oh, okay.

Cheryl Jacobs:

Yeah, I'm not a pink girl or flowers. Pink or flowers is not me.

AJ Mihrzad: By the way, what does a private jet go for nowadays? That's a big goal. I think everyone should aspire to own their own private jet.

Cheryl Jacobs:

You know what's crazy, though, too? It's probably going to be like a million dollars for your own private jet. The crazy thing about it is Tony Robbins talked about your time is more valuable than upping your private jet cost versus commercial. He told a story that he was invited to a dinner with important people and it took him 11 hours to get there, because he took commercial. When he got there, the guy was like, "Your time is more valuable than the cost of the private jet."

What Business Mastery had on it after that was like, "Okay, I'm looking for somebody to be a private jet." I literally put on there, "I'm a pilot. I have connections. I work with NetJets." I literally have two phone calls to make as soon as I'm done with here, because I literally am lining up private jet jobs. It's amazing.

AJ Mihrzad: Wow.

Cheryl Jacobs:

Proximity is power.

AJ Mihrzad: Yeah. You already made all the money back from your seminar and time away and all that stuff. That's phenomenal.

Cheryl Jacobs:

Yeah. Now I have to find the right assistant and I'm perfect. I'm golden. If I'm flying all over the place, I need somebody to be able to run this.

> **AJ Mihrzad:** Yeah, exactly. You're right or you want to leverage yourself.

Cheryl Jacobs:

Exactly. I'm getting overwhelmed, but I'll manage through it. Change my words and then you can change your mindset and you can do it.

> **AJ Mihrzad:** Exactly.

Cheryl Jacobs:

This is the truth.

> **AJ Mihrzad:** Yeah, everything will always fall into place. Yeah, you already have a lot of momentum. You're already very successful and it's just making those light tweaks.

Cheryl Jacobs:

Definitely. I have to get going, but I thank you so much for being on our show.

> **AJ Mihrzad:** Oh, my pleasure.

Cheryl Jacobs:

Oh, your podcast is Online Super Coach Podcast?

AJ Mihrzad: Yeah, that's the name of my company, Online Super Coach. There's a podcast. There's a seminar series, online training, book torrent it. If you just Google Online Super Coach, my website, you'll have everything on there, the podcast, the seminars, the retreats. I do a lot of free events. Now I'm doing them nationwide. By the time of this podcast, I'll have done it in different cities. If you're around, I would love to meet you.

Cheryl Jacobs:

Your Facebook is, what?

AJ Mihrzad: Facebook.com/ajfit, like fitness, A-J-F-I-T, and you will find me.

Cheryl Jacobs:

There you go. Well, thank you for appearing on the Kids Party Characters Podcast-

AJ Mihrzad: I'm honored.

Cheryl Jacobs:

... and pushing us to become the branding company and the membership site and everything like that.

AJ Mihrzad: Yes. I'm going to put this on my bio.

Cheryl Jacobs:

Yes. If I didn't meet you a year ago, I don't think I would be where I am right now, so I thank you from the bottom of my heart.

> **AJ Mihrzad:** I'm proud of you. You're working really hard and you inspire me, because all of your success and how far you've come since I've known you, that inspires me to go even harder, so thank you for that.

Cheryl Jacobs:

You're welcome. No more selfie queen.

> **AJ Mihrzad:** You're now the success queen, branding yourself and changing lives. That's amazing.

Cheryl Jacobs:

Yes, thank you. All right, AJ. Well, it was nice talking to you.

> **AJ Mihrzad:** Likewise, nice talking to you, too. This was fun. Thank you for having me.

Cheryl Jacobs:

You're welcome. I'll talk to you soon.

> **AJ Mihrzad:** All right, bye.

Bumi Veyg

Cheryl Jacobs:

Hello, welcome to Kids Party Characters Podcast. Make sure you subscribe on iTunes below. And today, I'd like to welcome on Bumi Veyg. I hope I said that right. He is a culinary school graduate who, while working in an industry, got a love for good science and product development. After years of self-teaching tasty food science, he began developing products to the market. He has built kettle corn factories, beverage manufacturing facilities, consulting on restaurants, factory production, marketing development and compliance. And he's currently working on launching several beverage brands, including a children's supplement line, and working on a distribution company called Master Beverages.

Hi, Bumi. How are you?

> **Bumi Veyg**: Hey, Cheryl. It's good to be here.

Cheryl Jacobs:

That was a mouth full.

> **Bumi Veyg**: Sorry. I should've worked less.

Cheryl Jacobs:

Should work less, no. No, that wouldn't be you then. No. Actually, the last time I spoke to you was, you got me in as a judge on the top model search in Jersey. So, the Awesome TV top model search in Jersey. So, you recommended me as a judge. That was basically the last time I seen you. So that was two months ago, right? At least.

> Bumi Veyg: That was December 1st, I believe.

Cheryl Jacobs:

Yeah, two months ago. So it looks you've been doing a lot since then.

> Bumi Veyg: Oh yeah, there's always something to do. I have to catch up to you.

Cheryl Jacobs:

Yeah, catch up to me. Yeah, I'm working on a flight club right now so I'm going to be flying far away from you soon.

> **Bumi Veyg:** No.

Cheryl Jacobs:

So, what got you into ... You're a chef, right, on the side? That's what you first started, as a chef?

Bumi Veyg: Yeah, I have a culinary degree. I don't professionally cook anymore. I cook more for friends and family as a hobby at this point, experiment with different things. But primarily what I do is, I develop and market beverages. And to give you an example, one of the beverages we're about to launch is a kid's shake called Bolder Kids by the Boulder Beverage Company. So this one here is a forest berry. I didn't pick it up for any particular reason other than just to show you the brand.

To tell you what it is, it's an organic and hypoallergenic shake for kids. So, there are no major allergens. It comes in four delicious flavors, which is a banana, forest berry, vanilla, and a whole bean chocolate shake. And the reason why we say whole bean chocolate shake is because we don't use any flavorings or extracts or concentrates in the chocolate one. All the flavor comes from cocoa powder and actual cocoa butter. So, I figured out a way to keep the cocoa butter malleable at room temperature without it going back to its hard state when it cools down. So all the flavor comes from the actual full cocoa products.

And it has fruits and vegetables and good fats from olive oil and prebiotics; not pro, but pre. Probiotics is the actual bacteria. Prebiotics is the thing that you need to sustain that bacteria. There is a lot of fiber relative to the other products on the market. It's a plan-based protein, about 7.2 grams per eight ounces. It comes from brown rice. And it's really a product that's made to be good for anybody.

Also, it's zero sugar. The sweeter comes from erythritol and stevia. Stevia is a all-natural sweetener. It comes from a plant, looks like tea. So, it's a far superior product than what's on the market currently. It's meant to be good for anybody. That's why I made sure when I formulated it, it would be zero sugar, a ton of 24 vitamins and minerals, good fats. For example, there's full synergy in the product. So, the banana one, the color comes from turmeric. Right?

Cheryl Jacobs:

So, there are anti-inflammatory benefits?

Bumi Veyg: Yeah, from turmeric and turmeric as we know is an amazing super food, but you can't just like, let's say you're to consume turmeric, your body will one absorb the curcumin that's in turmeric if you were to eat turmeric as is. You need some sort of catalyst, and that catalyst is pipeline, which is in black pepper. So, the banana has black pepper in there too, just enough for your body to absorb the curcumin in the turmeric.

And because of the good fats, fats also actually as an absorbent for nutrients, so your body will absorb the nutrients in the product much quicker. So, it's a full synergy, better for you, organic, hypoallergenic, non-GMO, vegan, Kosher, really ... It covers all the points.

Cheryl Jacobs:

Sounds like I would want to drink it.

>**Bumi Veyg:** Yeah, it's really good for anybody. Now, the funny thing is ... It's funny you mention that because we are going to do an adult version. Because it needs to be tweaked relative to the nutrients, but I did take it to ... There's a store called Natural Body Ink up here in New York, so their flagship store in Queens was throwing an event with a bunch of body builders, some really big names.
>
>I was like, "You know what? I'm going to be ballsy. And I'm going to take my kid shakes with me to take pictures with the body builders." So here I have these guys with their own products, right? And here I am, this little scrawny guy, relative to them with pictures of my product ...
>
>Yeah, and I'm taking pictures of my Bolder Kids and their products and them, and they're pointing at it like, "I love it. Can I have samples for myself because I would drink this?" I'm like, "Yeah, you could."

And they loved it, and because of the product, they still talk to me about, "Where can I buy it? Where can I get it?" Unfortunately, we're still not in production because we can't locate a co-packer. We have the funds necessary, and we have the product ready to go. But we're looking for a co-packer.

A co-packer is someone that produces a product for another company. It needs a very special production processing, and I'm still looking for one. So, one ...

Cheryl Jacobs:

Well, hopefully this platform will help get the word out there, and someone ...

Bumi Veyg: Yeah, I reached out to every single accepted co-packer in the country. If I have to go overseas, I will. I need to bring the products to market. People are requesting it. Schools are asking for it. Kids needs this. Kids are very picky eaters, and this gives them nutrition for the whole day, so ... I'm very eager to bring this to the market.

Parents need this kind of product.

Cheryl Jacobs:

Yeah, definitely. There's ... I'm not going to downgrade any products that are out there by name, but there's so many out there that are just full of sugar and not plant-based or ...

> **Bumi Veyg:** Or they're synthesized; they have soy, or they have dairy. It's not that they're not good for everybody, just a lot of them have synthesized ingredients, artificial flavors, and colors. And it's ... I tried to put together a full product that was good for anybody. Granted, if you're allergic to water, fruits and vegetables, you can't have it.

Cheryl Jacobs:

People are actually allergic to water?

> **Bumi Veyg:** Yeah, there's somebody allergic to something in the world. Believe it or not.

Cheryl Jacobs: Never heard of that before. That's so crazy.

> **Bumi Veyg:** So, it's hydrating too because it's water-based.

Cheryl Jacobs:

Yeah. So, I mean ... Have you ever considered Amazon? Does Amazon do distribution of those kinds of things, or no?

> **Bumi Veyg:** Yeah, I mean. We already have full distribution within New York City. If we wanted to go national, we could. We have the connections for that. We have the funds. Like I said, the only thing keeping us from producing product is finding the right production house to make the product for us.

But, eventually, I'll find one, and we'll be out there. All in due time, everything happens at the right time.

Cheryl Jacobs:

Yes, that's why I ...

Bumi Veyg: If it's meant to be, it'll be.

Cheryl Jacobs:

I created this platform to help everybody along the way because this is obviously going on iTunes, where the podcasts ... But it's also going on Facebook and Instagram and YouTube and LinkedIn. So, it's going all across the platforms, and ... I know you're on Facebook. What is your Facebook page?

Bumi Veyg: My Facebook page is my name: Bumi Veyg. You can ...

Cheryl Jacobs:

B-U-M-I V-E ...

Bumi Veyg: Yeah, B-U-M-I V-E-Y-G. We do have a Bolder Kids Facebook page too under the Boulder Beverage Company called The Boulder Beverage Company: B-O-U-L-D-E-R Beverage Company.

The brand is B-O-L-D-E-R. Like bolder, better, you know? It's a play on words, works really well. Our website is boulderbeverage.com. You can read up about the products. Hopefully, soon you'll be able to buy it off of the website. And then you mentioned Master Beverages, who's going to be our distribution company. We do have a Facebook page for that too: Master Beverage Inc.

The symbol is a old bottle cap with Master on it, so if you're going to look out for it, that's what it looks like. You can see all the brands we work with as well, and we work with really big brands, so ... There's a good base to this product, and there's a good base to the distribution for it.

Cheryl Jacobs:

Awesome, so, going back to the restaurant business, you're not going to do that anymore? You're not going to ...

> **Bumi Veyg:** No. Restaurant is ... You know, I did a lot of thinking about that. Because I'm a risk taker. You know this. I enjoy trying new things, trying new businesses and products. I'm a thinker. I create products all the time. And I was considering opening up a pasta-ria, a restaurant that was based on pasta. Fresh pasta, be able to do wholesale, and retail and all that stuff; and then between 9:00 p.m. and 11:00 p.m., do a la carte where people can sit down can come and sit down as a restaurant.

But I did the math, and the numbers did not justify opening up an establishment relative to marketing a product because it costs the same to open an establishment as it does to market a product within the first two years. But that marketed product could reach millions of people as opposed to an establishment, only 'X' amount of people through ...

Cheryl Jacobs:

Local.

Bumi Veyg: Traffic and driving and all that.

Cheryl Jacobs:

Yeah, it's local.

Bumi Veyg: I took the other route.

Cheryl Jacobs:

Yeah, I believe that the online marketing right now is the biggest thing that's out there right now anyway. It's kind of why I took my Kid's Party Character Company global is because being limited to New York, New Jersey, Connecticut; I wasn't going anywhere. I was making a profit, but I wasn't really going anywhere where I wanted to the next level.

So that's I opened Kid's Party Characters Global with the membership site, where people want to own their own territory and everything like that. And we open in Chicago and London this next month in March, so I'm traveling there with one of my actors and my sales route, so ... And one of my actors is going to dress like a princess every day or a super hero every day

Bumi Veyg: They're going to dress up like Cheryl Jacobs. From hero to princess.

Cheryl Jacobs:

Yeah, I'm debating if I'm going to dress up like a princess or a super hero with her or maybe a business suit. I'm not sure yet. I will try it both ways and see what works best. You know?

Bumi Veyg: Like walking into a meeting and drinking your own product. Like, "That's good. You should buy it. If I'm drinking it, you should buy it."

Cheryl Jacobs:

Called it.

Bumi Veyg: Exactly.

Cheryl Jacobs:

So ... All right, well, I mean ... It was so good talking to you. I'm so glad that we got this out here for you, and I hope that I can help you with distribution and marketing and all that kind of stuff. And I have my second book coming out too, which is Beyond the Enchanted, which will be on Amazon too, and you're definitely going to be included in that.

We're marketing for you, and hopefully, together we can make this grow.

> **Bumi Veyg:** Yeah, absolutely. We could easily put stuff on the label for you too. Let's say ... We can throw a giveaway, where under the cap, if you find the code, or you could figure out the riddle ...

Cheryl Jacobs:

Get a free kid party yourself.

> **Bumi Veyg:** Yeah, exactly. Get your kid's party by Kid's Party Characters.

Cheryl Jacobs:

There you go. That'll work.

> **Bumi Veyg:** Cross-pollination there too.

Cheryl Jacobs:

A little cross promotion.

> **Bumi Veyg:** Yeah, absolutely, it's what friends are for, helping each other out. Right?

Cheryl Jacobs:

So any big Valentine's Day plans for tomorrow?

> **Bumi Veyg:** Do I have any plans for ... You're putting me on the spot, Cheryl?

Cheryl Jacobs:

You don't have to answer that. I'm doing the single's night out with my girlfriends, so ... It'll be fun. That is my dog in the background, making all that noise. So I'm sorry about that. He's ...

> **Bumi Veyg:** That's fine.

Cheryl Jacobs:

So ...

> **Bumi Veyg:** He's a baby.

Cheryl Jacobs:

Yeah, he is.

Okay, so, I'm going to put all of your information for your Facebook page to get ahold of anybody that wants to find out more about your children's beverage products. And what is it called again? I'm sorry, Bolder ...

> **Bumi Veyg:** So, the company is Boulder Beverages, but the product lines is B-O-L-D-E-R. Bolder Kids.

Cheryl Jacobs:

Okay.

> **Bumi Veyg:** All that information is on our Facebook and on our website, and we do a really quick turnover if anybody, reaches out to us via our Facebook page. Within two to four hours, they will get a response.

Cheryl Jacobs:

Okay. Awesome. Well, it was good talking to you, and ...

> **Bumi Veyg:** Yeah, likewise. Thank you for the help.

Cheryl Jacobs:

Thanks for being on our Kid's Party Characters podcast.

> **Bumi Veyg:** Yeah, hopefully, I'll be back with better news, right? Like, "Oh, we launched!"

Cheryl Jacobs:

Yeah, our next interview will be like, "Oh my gosh, you've got us a marketing distributee or something. That would be amazing."

> **Bumi Veyg:** Yeah, and then we'll put you on the cap.

Cheryl Jacobs:

Distribution partner, or something, I don't know. Whatever you can call that.

> **Bumi Veyg:** We'll figure it out.

Cheryl Jacobs:

All right, well, thank you, Bumi, and have fun on Valentine's Day tomorrow.

> **Bumi Veyg:** Thank you.

Cheryl Jacobs:

Whatever your plans ...

Bumi Veyg: Thank you.

Cheryl Jacobs:

Thank you.

Cheryl Jacobs: Hi, I'm Cheryl Jacobs and welcome to Kids Party Characters Podcast. Make sure you subscribe below. Today we have an amazing author and my ghostwriter for my book, Escape From the Darkness Into the Enchanted. She also has a heart of gold. Hi Carla. How are you?

> **Carla Wynn Hall:** Hi Cheryl. I'm really, really good. Thank you for having me on your show. This is exciting. It's really time for me to start learning how to speak more on these videos and things like this. So this is a great opportunity.

Cheryl Jacobs:

Yeah. I know. I'm right here with you girl. I just started doing this myself, so we can hold each other's hand.

> **Carla Wynn Hall:** Okay.

Cheryl Jacobs:

You've written several books. How long have you been an author?

> **Carla Wynn Hall:** I wrote my first book, and you can see them behind me. I've got them cleverly positioned there for some shameless promotion. I actually started my first book in 2011 after what I call my very last rock-bottom experience.
>
> The Mayan conflict of 2011 just kind of stirred up my soul, and I was in a place where I knew that I needed to write my story. And if didn't, it was a good chance that I would forget what it even was about.

I started writing that book in 2011. I self published it in 2014. The book was really chronicling my journey up from my own abusive situation in 1990 up to that point in 2011. Then I learned about self-publishing, so I actually became an author in 2014. Since that time, I've published four of my own best-selling books, each over 300 pages.

Cheryl Jacobs:

Wow. I better step up. Mine's only 60 pages.

> **Carla Wynn Hall:** I'm addicted to it. I'm addicted to writing.

Cheryl Jacobs:

You are. Every time I see you on Facebook, I always say, "Oh my God, she's got another book coming out." I'm like this girl is amazing.

> **Carla Wynn Hall:** Thank you.

Cheryl Jacobs:

Thank you for really helping me with mine. I know my handwriting and all that was not probably the best for you to read.

> Carla Wynn Hall: I loved it though because I could see when you had a thought you'd scratch it out.

Cheryl Jacobs:

Yeah, and then once it starts coming out, it just starts coming out like in pages and pages.

Carla Wynn Hall: Yeah. I'm just proud that you did it.

Cheryl Jacobs:

Well I'm so glad that I met you. A mutual friend of ours, Mel Martin, introduced us. And I've been wanting to write my book forever. My book, for anybody that wants to know, it's Escape From the Darkness Into the Enchanted.

It's the story of a teenage mother who's living in poverty. A successful, nine-time business owner who found her passion in children's entertainment. And now I created the membership site for mothers, stay-at-home moms to have their own children's entertainment company through the comfort of their own homes.

That's what my book is about. It's my journey along the way and my struggles, bad relationships and everything that I've overcome. Yeah. Thank you for getting that out of me because it was an emotional journey, I must admit because you had me crying and talk about this and talk about that. We all hold things in, and it's not easy for you to get it out, but once you start getting it out, the words just start flowing.

Carla Wynn Hall: That's true.

Cheryl Jacobs:

Okay, and you also have your own children's book. Let's hear about this.

Carla Wynn Hall: Okay, well it's actually an author in Canada, her name is Marie Dahl, and she like you, presented us with some hand-drawn coloring sheets. Literally just things that she had colored over the years with crayons. We took her book and created a series of four books about a little fairy named Aksana. And Aksana was a shy fairy. She had friends. She had a little cousin, Daisy. They all come to help her get out into the world more.

Really, it's a children's book series about introverted and shy children, and how they can get out into the world a little bit more and open up their voices a little bit more. It's really based on her actual grand-niece. The little girl's name is Aksana. The characters in the book are based on Aksana's baby sister and Aksana's big brother. That's on Amazon.com under Aksana the Shy Fairy. You can find those hardback ... They're about 30 pages long, children's books.

Cheryl Jacobs:

Well those sound very inspirational for children who are shy. Maybe I should give those out at my kids parties. There's a couple of kids that will not come near the character at all.

You know you have those ones that are like hugging and high-fiving and everything else. Then you got those ones that are hiding behind their mom pretty much the whole time.

Carla Wynn Hall: When my husband was Santa Claus this year, we had the best time ever. But he found a niche with autistic children that I would have never guessed in a million years. Children who had not really ever spoken a lot to Santa Claus or anybody for that matter, just took to him. It was really shocking to see but, once he found that conversation piece, they latched onto him.

Cheryl Jacobs:

Yeah, I can imagine. A lot of times we do parties for autistic children, and it's like they have such a more of appreciation for the character or Santa Claus than normal. And it's pretty amazing.

I actually did Elmo one time for an autistic child, and I went above and beyond. I was helping the mother set up, everything, and the child loved Elmo so much, he did not eat his cake. He did not want his food. He did not want to play with the other kids. All he wanted to do is sit on Elmo's lap the whole time. Thank God I had a big Elmo head on because I was bawling underneath.

Carla Wynn Hall: Aw.

Cheryl Jacobs:

I was. I was like I'm going to send somebody else to do this next time because I can't handle it. Let me say, the parents were so appreciative after. They were like, thank you so much. My son really, really loved it, and they were like ... I'm sure that every year, they're gonna have us come back.

Carla Wynn Hall: Yeah. Absolutely.

Cheryl Jacobs:

I mentioned we were introduced by Mel Martin. Did Mel finish his book? Or he's about to finish his book? I don't even know.

> **Carla Wynn Hall:** I'm not exactly sure, but he's on his way. I mean I believe that some of these last things he's doing, he's putting into his book. So he's getting there.

Cheryl Jacobs:

Yeah, I actually interviewed him a couple of weeks ago, so he's gonna be on our podcast as well.

> **Carla Wynn Hall:** He's way more energetic than me. I can't keep up with that man.

Cheryl Jacobs:

You know what? I can't either, and he came to New York City for a visit, and he's like, Cheryl, let's go to the gym. Let's go do this. Let's do this. I'm sitting here behind my computer all day, and he's "Let's go. Let's go. Let's go." And he's in his 50s.

Then my poor dog. I have this fold-out couch, and my dog's not used to anybody being here because I live alone. Here's my dog in Mel's face. That's what he had to wake up to.

> **Carla Wynn Hall:** And you're going, "Oh."

Cheryl Jacobs:

Thank God that they bonded and liked each other because what a way to wake up.

> **Carla Wynn Hall:** Yeah. Well my dog is very protective of me too. He's super protective of me. It's crazy how you can bond with your animals though. But I call him my boyfriend. He's been with me for 10 years now, not left, not one time. I say that. He did. He left for three weeks one time, but I know what he was doing. They did not sue me for child support either. I'm just kidding.

Cheryl Jacobs:

I would probably say that they're better than a boyfriend. They're loyal. They don't cheat. You know. They love you unconditionally, better than a boyfriend. Better than any boyfriend I've ever had.

> **Carla Wynn Hall:** I hear you.

Cheryl Jacobs:

So your new book you just put out is Bending the Youniverse, Y-O-U universe. There you go. That's it.

> **Carla Wynn Hall:** It's little too. This is the littlest book I've ever done. It's a little one.

Cheryl Jacobs:

What's little? How many pages?

> **Carla Wynn Hall:** This one is 217 pages.

Cheryl Jacobs:

Oh my goodness. That's your little book.

>**Carla Wynn Hall:** Those behind me are each about 360 pages.

Cheryl Jacobs:

Oh my goodness. You go girl. That's amazing.

>**Carla Wynn Hall:** I'm a geek.

Cheryl Jacobs:

That's okay. This just got released on Amazon. Correct?

>**Carla Wynn Hall:** I released it on Christmas Day, actually, and it's available on Kindle and paperback right now. You all have to check out my one-star stalker review because everybody gets one. At least you know somebody's paying attention. This person put the same exact review on all of my books, copy/pasted it.
>
>Anyway, this book really, this is about taking everything that you think you know about life and just bending it. It validates the ego, and I think a lot of people don't do that. They want to toss out the ego. They want it to be something separate from them.

But the ego's a very strong personality within women. Sometimes that ego comes up, and she's actually like a protective personality. So I try to ease that boundary between seeing ego as bad and assimilating it back into who you are as a personality that has really helped you over the years through different things.

It talks about all these other modalities that you see, and how you can use them. But you don't have to be so attached to them that that becomes your only modality. I've watched you go through all sorts of different programs and things, and I see that you're really getting passionate now about the business part of everything and the Tony Robbins conferences and things like that.

So many people get madness from modalities, that they think that is exactly what they're supposed to always do and nothing different. So as I started looking at what was going on inside of me, I found that I've got this league of archetypes. It's like this guardian team of personalities that comes to me when I need them the most.

I've got an inner child that's wounded. I've got the soul of me, which makes me who I am. There's a mother polarity. There's a father polarity. Then there's that ego. She's taken the biggest hit because so many people say, "Don't be in your ego."

Well you know Tony Robbins, this is his philosophy. He says if he were gonna hire a sales person, she would have compassion and the ego energy to close sales despite hundreds of nos. So she could take a whole lot of NOs, and then turn it into a yes. He calls that ego energy.

So in trying to separate ego from women, they literally are trying to sever out parts of themselves to please other people. And because of that they don't have a grasp of who they are as a whole person. And it's taken me writing four books to finally get there.

Cheryl Jacobs:

Yeah. A couple of things. Tony Robbins actually did an example last week about how he gets his sales people. And he has this copy where he tells them that he wants somebody that's spectacular, who could take on anything, who's worth a million dollars in sales, and they have to sell themselves, basically. Then when they call, his staff is to be like, "That's not a million dollars." And then hang up on them.

The people who call back, like literally four times, are the ones who get hired because he says you have to be able to accept no. And you have to push past that barrier. That's one of the things that stuck out in my mind.

> **Carla Wynn Hall:** Exactly, exactly. The ones that are willing to go the distance and do it no matter what.

Cheryl Jacobs:

Along with your book too, you know you have to be true to yourself. If you're trying to be something you're not, it's not genuine. And people see right through it. That's the only way I think you can find happiness is to be your true genuine self. And when your true genuine self comes out, you get surrounded by the people that love you for who you are.

> **Carla Wynn Hall:** That's true. That's what I consider you to be too. Just so you know.

Cheryl Jacobs:

Well, I spent a lot of years trying to please everybody and make everybody happy. And you can't do it because you know, I had the one-star review on my book too. Here's my book everybody. Thanks to Carla, it's now out there on Amazon, and I have the one-star review. It was something like, "Oh my God, there was spelling errors."

> **Carla Wynn Hall:** That's the exact same comment that's on my book. I think it's the same person.

Cheryl Jacobs:

It's probably the same person. Your stalker is stalking me now. I'm like, oh God.

> Carla Wynn Hall: But you know what I did to counter that. I went and gave away 10 copies of the book to different people who I know, and I've asked them to come back and give their honest review. If I could comment on the comment that this person made, I would say, "I dare you to read my book." Because you'll see yourself written inside of my book. I know that they didn't read it because it wasn't a verified purchase. It made me a little bit uncomfortable at first, but then I just healed it because it's not even that important.

Cheryl Jacobs:

It's not that important because you know who you are. You know the people that love you know who you are, and there's always gonna be that one person who can't do what you're doing or doesn't have the guts to do what you're doing that's going to try and pull you down. There's always gonna be that one person.

> **Carla Wynn Hall:** Exactly.

Cheryl Jacobs:

Any plans for the future? Do you have any more books that you're working on. I know you just published one, but is there any more children's books?

Carla Wynn Hall: Actually, there's one book that I've started. It's gonna be about human potential, and it's gonna start with adults. And it's gonna be centered on parenting because I see so many new parents who need to know what's going on with their unborn children even while they're still in the womb. And I want to branch that out into a children's series on assertiveness and how right now, children are getting bullied. And by the way, I got to talk to both my grandkids over the last month or so on the phone.

Cheryl Jacobs:

Yay.

Carla Wynn Hall: That has opened up this space inside of me, and you know it was just hurting me so bad. But I've got in touch with the daughter-in-law, and I've been able to talk to both of them on video phone. It's so incredible. So my children's book series based on human potential is gonna be about how we can foster gentleness but assertiveness in children who are ages six to seven to eight because that's the most critical time for a child to learn.

They're absorbing everything as a sponge when they're three, four, five. They're taking everything in. But then they start processing it when they're seven, eight, and nine years old. They're starting to look at all these memories that they have of their mom and dad fighting. They're starting to process how it feels emotionally to them.

The human potential movement is gonna be my next book, but it's gonna go all the way from parents down into the children, up into the older generation now, so that we can see what we need to do to make this next jump. We're about to go into artificial intelligence, virtual reality. You've seen it. We've got so much already now that's not really humanized, so I want to re-humanize humanity. That is what I'm up to.

Cheryl Jacobs:

There was actually a woman who … I mean there is so many children too that it is such a crucial age. I think that's why I enjoy my business so much is because up until eight years old is what we really cater to, 1-8 year-olds. It's such a crucial time because they're still so innocent, and they're still not really corrupted yet, I guess you can say.

It's a great idea. I think there should be more programs too because all of us go into being a parent, there's no recipe for it. There's no instructions on it. You know, I think they should really have some more things out there, parenting groups or classes or something like that because the first one … They always say the first one you're so … They have that commercial. You're so protective of the first one, and you're like hand sanitizer and all this kind of stuff. Then the second one, you're just like, "Go play in the mud."

> **Carla Wynn Hall:** Yeah and the third one you're like… They'll make it.

Cheryl Jacobs:

The third one you're just like okay, can the older one watch the younger ones?

> **Carla Wynn Hall:** Yeah, I have three sons, so I went through everything any parent could go through. There were 10 years separation between my oldest son, Logan, and my middle son, Joshua. Then Nicholas was born five years after Joshua. So there's 15 years between Logan and Nicholas, which they never really got close at all. But with that gap and the fact that Logan's father actually was killed in 1990, it was hard to even know how to integrate them two as brothers.
>
> Yeah, but parents today, the moms when they're pregnant, when they're actually carrying the baby, this is when they need to be in programs that let them know how things like their emotions impact the baby. How some patterns that maybe they think is okay, like smoking when they're pregnant, how that impacts the baby.
>
> Because we're in a position now where we really can educate them. We can educate the new moms now, where when you and I were pregnant, there were no such thing as ultrasounds. You couldn't tell what your baby's sex was til you had it. And you had to kind of use your instinct. You had to use your mother instinct along the way. That's what you did.

But today, with the dawn of technology and all these things that we're learning about the DNA, energy patterns, things like that, new parents should be able to be educated now, even before they have the baby. Excuse me.

Cheryl Jacobs:

Yeah. I agree. I agree. There should be some kind of program out there. Back to what the woman from Tony Robbins, the Kyra Franchetti Foundation, I think everybody should look it up. It's a child who was murdered by her father because of a custody battle, then murdered himself and turned his house on fire as a way of revenge to get back at the mother of the baby, two years old.

And because of her foundation and her teaching everybody the importance of family and family values and things like that, she's got billboards now all over New York and L.A. and all across the globe right now.

There should be more educational things for parents, especially things parents with divorces and if they're fighting, and they're trying to work it out for the children's sakes, which I personally don't think is a good thing for children if they're being grown with that.

There's got to be some kind of education for parents and children out there somewhere. I think it should be more readily available.

Carla Wynn Hall: I agree.

Cheryl Jacobs:

I think it starts with the children because if they don't get it when they're small, it just brings it up into the adult world. There needs to be a change. That's gonna be my new mission maybe.

>**Carla Wynn Hall:** I'll do it with you.

Cheryl Jacobs:

There you go. I've actually started my second book that I'm gonna be sending over soon. I think I'll type it out for you this time, so you don't have to try and read my writing.

>**Carla Wynn Hall:** Okay.

Cheryl Jacobs:

But it's gonna be my journey from the kids company to the membership site where I teach stay-at-home moms to own their own children's entertainment company and the joy that goes along with it. It's gonna be my journey of all the experts that have helped me along the way like you and Mel and a bunch of the other people that have helped me along the way. Get ready girl because it's coming your way soon. Probably in a month or two.

>**Carla Wynn Hall:** I'm ready. I'm ready. You'll learn, and this is what I like to teach all the women that I work with, if you'll take every idea that you have, and you'll just start with the intention that it will be a book, you'll have book after book, easily.

Cheryl Jacobs:

Yeah, and everybody has a story. Everybody has a story to tell. Everybody's been through something. There is nobody that's had rainbows and flowers their whole life. Everybody has a story to tell, and let me tell you, it is the best therapy to write your own book and to get it out there. You're gonna cry along the way, and things that you put down inside yourself that you never wanted to talk about again, it releases it all. It really does.

I encourage people, if you want to write your book, Carla Wynn Hall is the woman to contact. She will help you all along the way.

> **Carla Wynn Hall:** Thank you.

Cheryl Jacobs:

There you go. Tell me where you are again. You're in Tennessee?

> Carla Wynn Hall: Where I am? I'm in Tennessee. Monteagle, Tennessee about 90 miles southeast of Nashville. I'm from Alabama, which is where this-

Cheryl Jacobs:

That's where the accent comes from?

> **Carla Wynn Hall:** Yeah.

Cheryl Jacobs:

I'm probably gonna start saying y'all now after talking to you.

Carla Wynn Hall: Y'all. Y'all. You gotta draw it out.

Cheryl Jacobs:

Tell everybody where we can reach you. What's your Facebook page?

Carla Wynn Hall: You can find me, Carla Wynn Hall on Facebook. It's Facebook.com/carlawynnhall, W-Y-N-N. Right now I have a program, that I'm starting. It's a free workshop, and it's at freedomthroughwriting.org. That's gonna be a seven-day workshop starting February 1, where I teach you how to create an outline for your book, how to start building your platform, then how to start your book launch.

My focus this year is building the Freedom Through Writing program, so that I can take it by the spring into prisons, rehab facilities for women, mental health facilities for women because just like Cheryl said, I believe that when you own this story enough to pull it out knowing that it's going to be a published book, that you go deeper into the healing.

Women by themselves can hide away stuff for years upon years upon years and never tell a soul. But that still lives inside of your body. That's freedomthroughwriting.org. I'm on Instagram as youniversebook, Y-O-U-niverse book, and everything else is Carla Wynn Hall, Twitter, LinkedIn. So all you would have to do is just type in my name.

I just want to encourage you, just like Cheryl said, if you have a story, even if you don't feel comfortable writing, even if you don't feel comfortable with a Word document, even if you really want to write it when you're the scaredest, under tent, on your bed, outside.

Just do it, and if you need help getting that into a book, let me know. I've constantly got programs going on where you could be a co-author and you just would submit one chapter. Or you can get with me, and I'll coach you all the way through putting a book out.

Cheryl Jacobs:

Yeah, that's what she did with me. Coached me, write about this. Write about that. And there's also apps too that you can download on your phone. I don't know them right now. I'll put it at the comments below. But there's apps that you can just talk right into your phone. You can tell your story daily. If something pops into your head, and you don't have a piece of paper and pen, just record it right into your phone. It's amazing. There's so many things right now that you can do.

That's about it. It's so nice to talk to you again, and I'm definitely gonna come visit you in Tennessee.

> **Carla Wynn Hall:** That would be fun. I could show you the mountains of nowhere, just mountains upon mountains, upon mountains. There's a place up here called High Point, and it's a restaurant that's situated on the summit between Chicago and Miami, it's directly in the center. That's such a beautiful restaurant, great place for a photo shoot if you ever want to come see the mountains.

Cheryl Jacobs:

I was actually in Knoxville before. Is that close to you, or no?

> **Carla Wynn Hall:** Knoxville's on the other side of Tennessee. It's closer to Gatlinburg and all that.

Cheryl Jacobs:

Okay. Well I came during the winter, so I'll come in the summer.

> **Carla Wynn Hall:** Okay.

Cheryl Jacobs:

I grew up in Ohio, so enough snow for me in Ohio.

> **Carla Wynn Hall:** That sounds good. I hear you. Thank you so much.

Cheryl Jacobs:

You're welcome Carla, and it was nice talking to you again.

> Carla Wynn Hall: Just let me know whenever everything's ready, and I'll share away.

Cheryl Jacobs:

There you go mama.

> **Carla Wynn Hall:** Bye-bye.

Cheryl Jacobs:

Bye.

DJ Dove

Cheryl Jacobs:

Hi, welcome to Kids Party Characters Podcast. Today we have a special guest, DJ Dove. I met him back when he was DJing for the Made in Italy parties in New York City. I used to help manage and promote his shows in New York City, Miami, Rome, and I'm sure there's a couple other places that he's been that I don't even know about. So let's welcome on DJ Dove.

> DJ Dove: Hey, what's going on? How's everybody? How are you, Cheryl?

Cheryl Jacobs:

I'm good. I'm glad the New Year is over and we can start moving forward on life, basically. So have you DJ-ed in other places? I don't even know. I haven't spoken to you in awhile.

> DJ Dove: Wow, I mean yeah. I mean, where haven't I been? I mean, I've been pretty much everywhere in Europe except a few places, but you know, I've been busy over the years. I took a bit of a sabbatical for awhile, for about a year and a half. I left the industry for a little bit and finished college and everything; went back and got my degree, and now I'm back.

Cheryl Jacobs:

You did Ibiza once, didn't you? Or no?

> DJ Dove: Yeah, I did it twice actually. The first time being in 2000.

Cheryl Jacobs:

That's on my bucket list. I want to go to Ibiza. Maybe start Kids Party Characters over there.

> DJ Dove: Yeah, of course. You're gonna have to learn a little bit of Spanish though.

Cheryl Jacobs:

I'll just bring a translator. I'll bring you! You can speak Spanish, no? No you can't, right?

> DJ Dove: Yeah, of course. Yeah, of course! I'm Cuban; my parents are from Cuba. I speak Spanish pretty fluently.

Cheryl Jacobs:

There you go. So you can go be my translator and I'll watch you spin.

> DJ Dove: That's it.

Cheryl Jacobs:

So, I mean, and you also currently have a show on Facebook, correct?

DJ Dove: Yes, it's called the DJ Dove Mastermix Sessions. I do it every Wednesday from 7 to 8:30 now. I used to do it from 7 to 8, but I extended it an extra half an hour, just because of the responses. I started it in July up until now have been amazing. So it's probably the best thing I could have ever did to expand my brand and stuff.

Cheryl Jacobs:

I know you're always sending me the links and I'm always like trying to tune in, but then I do for like a second and then I have to go do something else. But I know you're an amazing DJ; I mean, you did our intro and our outro for the podcast.

DJ Dove: Yes, which I hope it was to your liking.

Cheryl Jacobs:

Yes, I do like it. I sent it over to my podcast editor. It's all kind of up to him too. He's-

DJ Dove: Oh, podcast editor. Okay.

Cheryl Jacobs:

Yeah. He's coaching me through this whole process here.

DJ Dove: That's awesome.

Cheryl Jacobs:

Yeah. So how long have we known each other? I mean, we've known each other since like 2005, I think.

> DJ Dove: I believe we've known each other since 2006, because I remember meeting you at a Made in Italy party actually. It was the Made in Italy Halloween Party, which I believe it was either in 2006 or in 2007, because Aritzia and I were the DJs that night and you actually came. So that's how I met you.

Cheryl Jacobs:

Was I in costume? I don't remember.

> DJ Dove: Kinda, sort of.

Cheryl Jacobs:

I think I was a race car driver, right? Was I a race car driver?

> DJ Dove: Yeah, exactly.

Cheryl Jacobs:

Okay. Yeah, I can't exactly wear that one for a kid's party characters, but I remember that one. That's one of my favorites. It's so comfortable, so I used to love it.

So I mean, out of all these ... I mean, I managed DJs for like five years. Of all 50+ DJs, one of the few people who's actually stayed in touch, and kept your head on straight, and kept moving forward. So tell me what else have you been up to? I haven't really spoken to you.

> DJ Dove: You know, just basically getting back in the swing of things with music, because I got so frustrated with the industry after awhile. I said you know what, it's time to do something different for a little while; put the music on the back burner and just go back to something that's kind of been haunting me for a long time, and that was finishing my education.
>
> So I said you know what, this is a good time to do it. So I went back and I got my Bachelor's degree in business administration. Once I got that done, it was a major weight off me, because I was in and out when it comes to college and then I stood out for a long time. And I said you know what, it's time to get it done. And I finally got it done and nobody can take that away from me.

Cheryl Jacobs:

Yeah, that piece of paper. Once you get it, it's ... Sometimes you just have to take those three steps back to move a few steps forward, and it pays off. I mean, it took me a good six years to get all my licenses for my pilot license, you know? And I finally did it and I actually flew myself, as Elsa, to Boston for my girlfriend's niece's birthday, and she dressed up like Ana and we went over to do a little party in Boston. Which, you know ... Probably won't do it again, but it was a good experience.

>DJ Dove: That's so cool.

Cheryl Jacobs:

Yeah. And so I loved the intro that you did. I'm looking forward to putting it together with everything, and this is all a new experience, you know? If you want to be on in the future, just let me know, and let everybody know exactly where they can meet you as well, or hear you. What's your Facebook page and Instagram and all that kind of thing?

> DJ Dove: Let's see, my Instagram is DJDove33. That's also my Twitter and my YouTube channel as well, which you know, since I've been back in the swing of things, I'm putting the factory together slowly but surely, because I was away for a pretty long period of time. I don't regret going back to get my education, but when you're out of sight, out of mind for a bit and you come back, the transition is very difficult. But ever since I've been back ... It's been a slow process, but it's been improving more and more. So it feels good.

Also my website is DJDove.com. My Facebook is DJDoveHouseMusic1; that's my musician and band page. So yeah, definitely check me out.

Cheryl Jacobs:

Okay, most of it's so hard after ... It's probably like starting all over again when you take time off and come back. I mean-

> DJ Dove: Absolutely, because when you're gone for that long period of time ... You know better than anyone; the industry fluctuates. It changes every couple years as a new breed of people that you got to reach out to and get yourself familiar with, and there are some that are still around that know who you are, but you're just like ... You know, you gotta re-prove yourself again.

Cheryl Jacobs:

And it's a new generation too on top of it.

> DJ Dove: Yeah, new generation, new scene of people that want to hear a certain type of music. It's about adapting and knowing how to play the game, you know?

Cheryl Jacobs:

So what else? Anything else? Did you miss me? I haven't seen you in forever actually.

> DJ Dove: Yeah, it's been a couple of years since I seen you. The last time I think I saw you was at an event of mine and-

Cheryl Jacobs:

In Elizabeth, right? I went to see you in Elizabeth.

> DJ Dove: Right, right. Yes, that was the last time we saw each other. It's bee... Yeah, it has to be a couple years. And you look fantastic. I try to keep up with everything that you do, and like I said, I'm very proud of you. Very, very proud of you. From where you came from and where you're at now has been a major, major transition, and I'm very proud of you.

Cheryl Jacobs:

Yeah. When I stopped Manage DJs ... Thank you, I appreciate it. I mean, when I stopped Manage DJs, I was kind of in a limbo; like what do I do? What do I do with my life? And the Kids Party Characters just kinda fell in my lap.

I had an agent ... I was doing acting, modeling, dancing. I had an agent call me and ask me to play Cinderella at a kid's party and I was just like, "I don't know. I don't have little kids. I don't know how to talk to them." I literally talked to them like adults at first; like "Hey, what's up? How are you?"

And after awhile, I learned how to talk to them and listen to them, and hear them, and realize that they're little people and they have so much ... They're definitely are unfiltered; they have no filter, children have no filter.

You get at that age between two and three where they repeat everything you say, so you have to be careful.

> DJ Dove: Just as bad as adults.

Cheryl Jacobs:

Well, yeah. It's true. But they do that behind your back, I think. And I never ... Like the rest is history, you know? From there it went to the second party, to ending up working for him for two years, and then going on my own.

So happy that I did. I mean, I do miss the DJ business, don't get me wrong; I mean, going around New York City, Miami, Rome, wherever. Taking all my girlfriends, getting everybody in for free, the scene, all that kind of stuff. It was fun. But then sometimes you have to be an adult and grow up. Be responsible. I do miss it though, but I have no regrets. It taught me a lot, I met a lot of people like you yourself. You know, the lifetime friends.

> DJ Dove: I will always be here for you. You know that.

Cheryl Jacobs:

Yeah, and definitely when I get more time, we're gonna ... I'll come to one of your shows again and support you.

> DJ Dove: Well yeah. I'm gonna make sure I bring a Sharpie so then, you know, you can sign my shirt or whatever needs to be signed.

Cheryl Jacobs:

Well I hope this business gets so big that everybody knows the word "Kids Party Characters" and, you know ...

DJ Dove: Well now you're making a big contribution. Kudos to you.

Cheryl Jacobs:

Thank you.

So that's about it, and let me know when your next show is. I'll try and get a ... Even if I don't answer right away, you know I will soon. I'll definitely make it out. I mean, this podcast launches January 31st, which I probably shouldn't have said because by the time this is on the air, it's probably gonna be after that. But, you know, anybody that wants to come to our website, it's KidsPartyCharacters.com, or if you want to own your own Kids Party Characters franchise, we can help you with that too. And thank you, my friend DJ Dove, for coming on, and I cannot wait to launch us off with your music and come see you spin really soon.

DJ Dove: An absolute pleasure, thank you. Thank you for making me part of this. I'm truly honored.

Jose Baez

Cheryl Jacobs:

Hi. I'm Cheryl Jacobs, and welcome our Kids Party Characters podcast. Make sure you subscribe below. Today we have one of our top actors who started with us from the beginning. He's an actor with the New York Film Academy. He's a runway fashion model from the Dominican Republic. Please welcome, I know I'm going to say this wrong, Jose Baez.

> Jose Baez: Hey. How are you guys?

Cheryl Jacobs:

Did I say that right?

> Jose Baez: Yeah, of course. You say it perfectly.

Cheryl Jacobs:

Okay. You studied at the New York Film Academy, correct?

> Jose Baez: Yes. I did, yeah.

Cheryl Jacobs:

Are there other places that you've studied acting?

> Jose Baez: I was studying in Miami for a soap opera, but I was in an actors academy, that's for Spanish soap opera, and I was doing more jobs in Dominican Republic and studying as well.

Cheryl Jacobs:

So, is there a place that we can look for you? I mean, I'm sure you have appeared in things that we can ... Is there anything that we can look for you at that's published right now?

>Jose Baez: Yeah. We can go for mbmodelsacademy.com you can find my profile. Mbmodels.com.

Cheryl Jacobs:

That's where your portfolio is?

>Jose Baez: Yes. We got a lot of pictures there.

Cheryl Jacobs:

There you go. There you go ladies. So, are you pursuing more TV and film, or do you see yourself more in like, theater work?

>Jose Baez: I think TV is more for me. I'd be working a lot of TV shows, TV series, and movies, and this is my area I feel comfortable doing that area.

Cheryl Jacobs:

Yeah. I see you more in that like, and-

>Jose Baez: Yeah, the face.

Cheryl Jacobs:

Definitely like that and the print modeling, well, obviously you're tall enough to do the runway as well. So, you're also yeah, you're also the runway fashion model.

I know you've worked in New York City, is there other places that you've done your modeling work at?

> Jose Baez: Yeah I was in a lot of New York fashion shows, New York fashion week. I was working in some print campaigns, and-

Cheryl Jacobs:

And then they are what-

> Jose Baez: And commercial.

Cheryl Jacobs:

What's the name of the print campaigns and the fashion shows?

> Jose Baez: I was working for a lot of fashion shows in New York City, and a lot of designers. Well, I was working with Madonna in a video with Nicki Minaj. The name of the song is Bitch I'm Madonna.

Cheryl Jacobs:

I know that song.

> Jose Baez: Yeah, so I was working with Madonna as a bartender, and it was an experience. And I was working with Carol for cologne for men, so it was a great job there.

Cheryl Jacobs:

Nice.

> Jose Baez: And that was incredible, amazing, yeah. I can do a lot of jobs in New York, and New York has a lot of opportunities, so I feel happy to be here.

Cheryl Jacobs:

And you obviously you did ... You started obviously in Dominican Republic where you're from?

> Jose Baez: Yeah, yes. I started there working as a top model, and doing the same thing ad campaigns, print, then I came to United States and I started doing the same job here but with more opportunities, so now I feel happy, yeah.

Cheryl Jacobs:

Yeah, New York definitely has a lot of opportunities that's why I moved here from Ohio. A lot more opportunities out here, and I recently was a judge in Awesome Top Model search, which the first person I asked if they knew anybody to contact-

> Jose Baez: Yeah.

Cheryl Jacobs:

With that was you, and you did an amazing job. You got third place.

> Jose Baez: Thank you, thank you. That was amazing.

Cheryl Jacobs:

Yeah, and I have all those pictures and videos on my Facebook page, Cheryl Jacobs if you want to see that, girls, he's there. And you appeared out of 30 guys, so you got third place.

> Jose Baez: That's good, I was so happy, I was so prepared to develop a job in the opportunity, I did a great job. I feel happy to me, yeah.

Cheryl Jacobs:

Yeah, and also appeared on over 300 channels across the US and I think they had you come there at like, 10 a.m., right? And the show wasn't until like, 9 o'clock at night?

> Jose Baez: Yeah. It was a long day, it was amazing.

Cheryl Jacobs:

Yeah, they told me like, "Make sure he's there at 10 a.m." I'm like, I'm not going there at 10 a.m. I'm like, what time do you need me there? Because I was not gonna be there all day.

So, what did they do? They had you practice the runway show and everything-

> Jose Baez: Exactly. We would practice it the runways, then fitting the clothes, and teach us how to do the job. But I already know what I was supposed to do, and what was very confused to me in the beginning, but then I finally did the right way and we did a nice runway, yeah. Other guys, very nice costume, nice clothes, and it was incredible, yeah.

Cheryl Jacobs:

Yeah, me and the girl next to me had a good time. She kept elbowing me like, "Look at that one. Look at that one."

> Jose Baez: Yeah, had to do some pushup before I go out, yeah.

Cheryl Jacobs:

Yeah, it was fun for us, too. So, you ... Okay, so our company obviously started four years ago, Kids Party Characters started four years ago here in New York City, New Jersey, Connecticut area, and as we expanded because we started with the two or three characters every weekend and now we're up to 20 or 30. You were one of the first actors that we casted.

So, I believe you played a superhero first. I can't even remember. That was like, four years ago.

> Jose Baez: I think it was Batman or something like this, yeah.

Cheryl Jacobs:

Batman, yeah. So, the first time going into it, what did you do? Because I'm curious to know-

> Jose Baez: Well, first of all when I met you before I got my job. I said, "Wow she's a beautiful lady. I think she's an actor or something like this because ..." And then when I started doing my job my first time there was as Batman, I searched a little bit online. I was studying the actor, so when I went there I jump from the house to the backyard as a Batman, and yeah, it was crazy, but the kids they were so happy.
>
> I was supposed to do balloons, and that was my first time. I tried to do it, but I only did swords, and at the end of the day the kids they were so happy with me, and I found that this job is a good way to release the stress, to be happy, and to see how we make other people happy. So, it's an amazing job. I love it every time I spend with the kids, and that's what I like to do.

Cheryl Jacobs:

Yeah, it's definitely an instant mood booster, that's for sure. You know, as happy as these kids get is probably why I think I found my passion with this business. Other than all the other businesses you know, this is my ninth business, but this is the one that I found my passion in, and so, now parties now, so what do you think the difference is now that you go into these parties now that you're-

> Jose Baez: Now, before I get there before I get to every party I know what I have to do, and I have ... I believe in myself now more than before because I found a way to make kids happy. I got the songs, I can do balloons when they custom, I can do balloons without seeing the balloon-

Cheryl Jacobs:

I don't know how ... I've seen you do that-

> Jose Baez: Yeah.

Cheryl Jacobs:

With your costume on that you can barely see out of. Even the mothers have come up to me and like, "That is amazing that he can do that with this costume on" you know, because not all of my actors can do that.

> Jose Baez: I try to do as much as I can because when I do my job for example, as Elmo, or Marshall, and I do balloons I see with the kids on the floor, and I try to do flowers, puppy, sword, hat, heart, a lot of things. Kids say, "Wow! He's real! Oh my God!" And so they appreciate more my time, and I spend more time with the custom with the kids, so it's a good way to make this job more real.

Cheryl Jacobs:

Yeah. I'm still amazed that you can do that because I've never been able to do that-

Jose Baez: Just practice, just practice.

Cheryl Jacobs:

I know, I've literally tried it sitting on the floor with Minnie Mouse and the Minnie Mouse head, and I've had to sit down when I do it because I tried it once, and I don't know how you do it, but it's amazing that you can do it with that costume on. Okay, so-

Jose Baez: Yeah.

Cheryl Jacobs:

So, any actors that would like to work in this kind of business, what advice do you have for them?

Jose Baez: Well, my advice is this is a great opportunity to grow up as an actor because you will develop different actors, different kind of a personalities, like Spiderman, Batman, Hulk, so this is a great opportunity to grow up, and we as an actor, we found this job like, the best job ever. So, when we find the best way to make other happy, I think this is the meaning of the life.

Cheryl Jacobs:

Yeah, and I think it's amazing that when you actors go in there and like, some of my actors can go in there and sing Let it Go and they have these soprano voices, and I'm on the sidelines just recording them and you know.

Because mothers do ask for that, and it's great that you guys all immerse yourself into that character, and become that character because you know, there's always that one kid who's like, "

Oh you're not the real Spiderman," or whatever. But when you know your character, and you know how to act like your character then you can even get the most skeptical kids to believe, and that's I think probably one of the most amazing things about this business. So ...

Jose Baez: Exactly.

Cheryl Jacobs:

And you know-

Jose Baez: Exactly, that's-

Cheryl Jacobs:

And now you have all these friends that you've kind of like, I know you're like, "Cheryl I have this friend that wants to do it, I have this friend to do it." So I mean, I can tell you love it, and I'm so glad that we have you on board with us, and watching us grow from where we were to two to three parties over the weekend-

Jose Baez: From the beginning, yeah.

Cheryl Jacobs:

Yeah, and to where we are now.

Now we're branching globally, and I'm teaching all these women, you know, if they want to own their own children's entertainment company you know, they can gain financial freedom through the comfort of their own home, so anybody interested in hat, you just go to Kids Party Characters and click on members if you want to learn more about that, and where can we find you?

Do you have any upcoming jobs or anything like that that we should look for you in? Or you're acting, or modeling? Are you still with the New York Film Academy?

> Jose Baez: I'm still working, I'm still doing a lot of jobs, and this is ... If you're an actor, and you are in New York I'll tell you that keep going working hard, keep focused because life sometimes is hard, but at the end of the day we're gonna find the best way to find success and the meaning. New York, United States, and around the world we have a lot of opportunities. We need to focus, and work hard.

Cheryl Jacobs:

Yes, definitely. Yeah, and especially with this job you know, I was an actor, model for many years, so before I got into this business. So I think this is a great way for you know, struggling actors or models to make a great living on the weekend. It's a couple days a weekend, and so anybody that wants you know, looking for work, actors, models-

> Jose Baez: Exactly.

Cheryl Jacobs:

You know-

> Jose Baez: And-

Cheryl Jacobs:

I got Jose over there who's my reference.

> Jose Baez: You got me, you got me, yeah. So, I can teach you, yeah of course.

Cheryl Jacobs:

And what is your Facebook page so people can find you? It's ...

> Jose Baez: You can find me ... It's Jose, J-O-S-E, Emilio, E-M-I-L-I-O, Baez, B-A-E-T-Z. Jose Emilio Baez on Facebook, and Instagram you can find me as joseemilio_1. Joseemeilio_1. You will find me there and I'll be happy to follow you back, yeah.

Cheryl Jacobs:

There you go. Well, thank you so much Jose for being on the show, and I look forward to growing this business-

> Jose Baez: Thank you, too.

Cheryl Jacobs:

To the next level with you, and-

> Jose Baez: Let's do it, yeah.

Cheryl Jacobs:

We're on board. So, Kids Party Characters podcast, make sure everybody subscribes below, and have a great day Jose, nice talking to you.

> Jose Baez: And thank you so much for the opportunity, all right. Thank you guys for watching us, bye-bye.

www.ingramcontent.com/pod-product-compliance
Lightning Source LLC
Chambersburg PA
CBHW052259220526
45471CB00001B/401